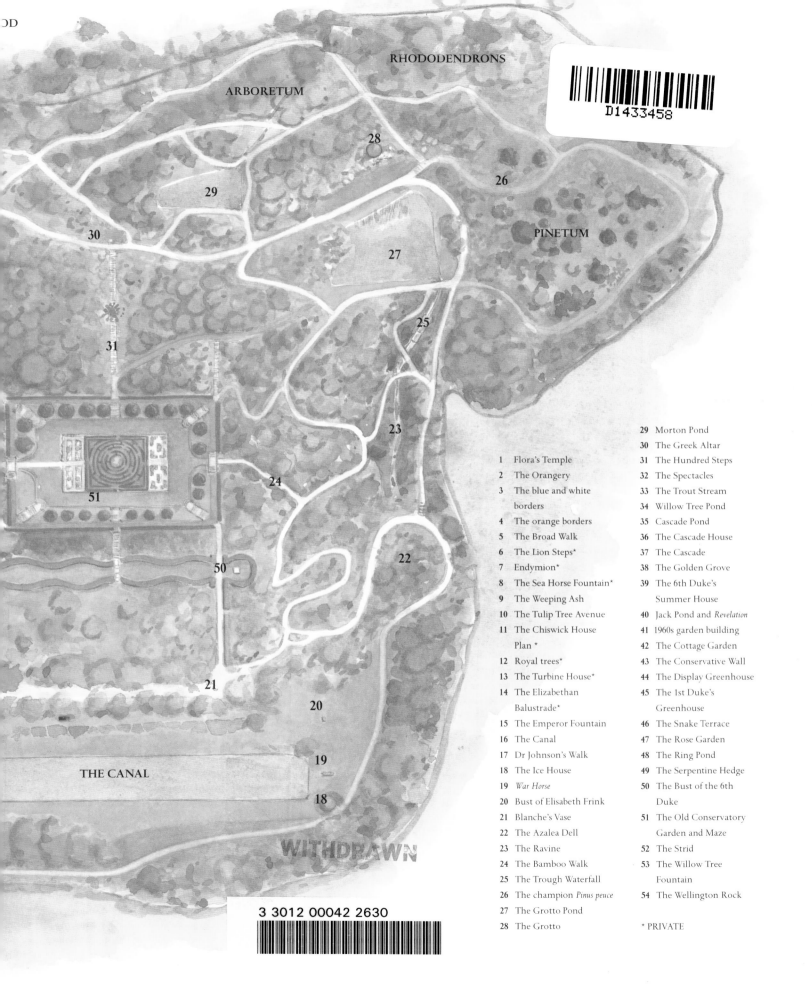

ARBORETUM

RHODODENDRONS

PINETUM

THE CANAL

1 Flora's Temple
2 The Orangery
3 The blue and white
   borders
4 The orange borders
5 The Broad Walk
6 The Lion Steps*
7 Endymion*
8 The Sea Horse Fountain*
9 The Weeping Ash
10 The Tulip Tree Avenue
11 The Chiswick House
   Plan *
12 Royal trees*
13 The Turbine House*
14 The Elizabethan
   Balustrade*
15 The Emperor Fountain
16 The Canal
17 Dr Johnson's Walk
18 The Ice House
19 War Horse
20 Bust of Elisabeth Frink
21 Blanche's Vase
22 The Azalea Dell
23 The Ravine
24 The Bamboo Walk
25 The Trough Waterfall
26 The champion Pinus peuce
27 The Grotto Pond
28 The Grotto

29 Morton Pond
30 The Greek Altar
31 The Hundred Steps
32 The Spectacles
33 The Trout Stream
34 Willow Tree Pond
35 Cascade Pond
36 The Cascade House
37 The Cascade
38 The Golden Grove
39 The 6th Duke's
   Summer House
40 Jack Pond and Revelation
41 1960s garden building
42 The Cottage Garden
43 The Conservative Wall
44 The Display Greenhouse
45 The 1st Duke's
   Greenhouse
46 The Snake Terrace
47 The Rose Garden
48 The Ring Pond
49 The Serpentine Hedge
50 The Bust of the 6th
   Duke
51 The Old Conservatory
   Garden and Maze
52 The Strid
53 The Willow Tree
   Fountain
54 The Wellington Rock

* PRIVATE

Dedicated to the memory of Bert Link,
to his son Jim
and all the Chatsworth gardeners
past and present

THE GARDEN AT

THE DUCHESS OF

Photographs by
Gary Rogers

CHATSWORTH

DEVONSHIRE

FRANCES
LINCOLN

Frances Lincoln Limited
4 Torriano Mews, Torriano Avenue
London NW5 2RZ

The Duchess of Devonshire: The Garden at
Chatsworth
Copyright © Frances Lincoln Limited 1999
Text copyright © The Duchess of Devonshire 1999
Photographs copyright © Gary Rogers 1999
unless otherwise credited on page 192

First Frances Lincoln edition: 1999

British Library Cataloguing in Publication data.
A catalogue record for this book is available from
the British Library

ISBN 07112 1430 1

Printed in Hong Kong
9 8 7 6 5 4 3 2

Page 1 The yew maze
Pages 2–3 A border in the West Garden
This page One of the marble figures on the Broad Walk

Contents

The Cavendish Family

1505–1557 Sir William Cavendish = Bess of Hardwick *c.* 1527–1608
son of Thomas Cavendish of Suffolk   *later Countess of Shrewsbury*

1552–1625 William Cavendish = Anne Keighley *d.* 1625
1ST EARL OF DEVONSHIRE (1618)   *dau. of Henry Keighley*

1590–1628 William Cavendish = Hon. Christian Bruce 1595–1675
2ND EARL OF DEVONSHIRE   *dau. of 1st Lord Kinloss*

1617–1684 William Cavendish = Lady Elizabeth Cecil 1619–1689
3RD EARL OF DEVONSHIRE   *dau. of the 2nd Earl of Salisbury*

1640–1707 William Cavendish = Lady Mary Butler 1646–1710
4TH EARL OF DEVONSHIRE   *dau. of the 1st Duke of Ormonde*
1ST DUKE OF DEVONSHIRE (1694)

1673–1729 William Cavendish = Hon. Rachel Russell 1674–1725
2ND DUKE OF DEVONSHIRE   *dau. of William Lord Russell*

1698–1755 William Cavendish = Catherine Hoskins *d.* 1777
3RD DUKE OF DEVONSHIRE   *dau. of John Hoskins*

Lord Charles Cavendish *d.* 1783 = Lady Anne Grey *d.* 1733
dau. of the Duke of Kent

1720–1764 William Cavendish = Lady Charlotte Boyle 1731–1754
4TH DUKE OF DEVONSHIRE   *dau. of the 4th Earl of Cork and 3rd Earl of Burlington; estates in Yorkshire and Ireland, Chiswick House, Burlington House*

1731–1810 Henry Cavendish *the scientist*

1757–1806 (1) Lady Georgiana Spencer = William Cavendish 1748–1811 = (2) Lady Elizabeth Foster
dau. of the 1st Earl Spencer   5TH DUKE OF DEVONSHIRE   (née Hervey) 1757–1824
dau. of the 4th Earl of Bristol

1754–1834 Lord George Cavendish = Lady Elizabeth Compton 1760–1835
1st Earl of Burlington (2nd creation)   *heiress to the 7th Earl of Northampton; estates in Sussex*

1790–1858 William Spencer Cavendish
6TH DUKE OF DEVONSHIRE

Lady Georgiana Cavendish = George Howard 1773–1848
1783–1858   *6th Earl of Carlisle*

1783–1812 William Cavendish = Hon. Louisa O'Callaghan *d.* 1863
killed in carriage accident   *dau. of the 1st Lord Lismore*

1803–1881 Lady Caroline Howard = Rt Hon. William Lascelles 1798–1851
son of the 2nd Earl of Harewood

1812–1840 Lady Blanche Howard = William Cavendish 1808–1891
2nd Earl of Burlington (2nd creation)
7TH DUKE OF DEVONSHIRE

1838–1920 Emma Lascelles = Lord Edward Cavendish 1838–1891

1833–1908 Spencer Compton Cavendish = Countess Louise von Alten 1832–1911
8TH DUKE OF DEVONSHIRE   *'The Double Duchess': formerly Duchess of Manchester*

1868–1938 Victor Cavendish = Lady Evelyn Fitzmaurice 1870–1960
9TH DUKE OF DEVONSHIRE   *dau. of the 5th Marquess of Lansdowne*

1895–1950 Edward Cavendish = Lady Mary Cecil 1895–1988
10TH DUKE OF DEVONSHIRE   *dau. of the 4th Marquess of Salisbury*

b. 1920 Andrew Cavendish = Hon. Deborah Mitford *b.* 1920
11TH DUKE OF DEVONSHIRE   *dau. of the 2nd Lord Redesdale*

1917–1944 William Cavendish = Kathleen Kennedy 1920–1948
Marquess of Hartington   killed in action   *sister of President Kennedy*

b. 1944 Peregrine Cavendish = Amanda Heywood-Lonsdale *b.* 1944
Marquess of Hartington

Lady Emma Cavendish *b.* 1943 = Hon. Tobias Tennant
son of the 2nd Lord Glenconner

b. 1969 William Cavendish
Earl of Burlington

Lady Celina Cavendish *b.* 1971 = Alexander Carter

Lady Jasmine Cavendish *b.* 1973

Lady Sophia Cavendish *b.* 1957 = (1) Anthony Murphy
(2) Alastair Morrison

Isabel Tennant *b.* 1964 = Piers Hill   Edward Tennant *b.* 1967   Stella Tennant *b.* 1970   Declan Morrison *b.* 1993   Nancy Morrison *b.* 1995

Preface

Not long ago I was asked to write an article for the first issue of a new gardening magazine. The subject was 'My Favourite Gardening Book'. The magazine sank without trace and without warning but, by the time I realised it was not wanted, I had cast about for what I was supposed to describe. I found so many gardening books that I was overwhelmed. They become brighter, fatter and heavier by the month: enough to fill every potting shed shelf from here to eternity.

I apologise for adding yet one more. My excuse for doing so is that the garden I have known from dawn to dusk for fifty years owes its existence to masters and men of exceptional talent. They created 'the Duke of Devonshire's Elysian fields' to please anyone who cares to come here, and it may be of use to future generations for the stories of their achievements to be gathered into a single volume.

No one person designed the garden at Chatsworth. It has evolved according to the taste of successive Dukes of Devonshire unshackled by committees. Every style of gardening has been tried; some have survived and some have disappeared. Fashion has played a part, as it inevitably does. At Chatsworth it has often been a case of leading rather than following the trend. Several times the landscape was changed as if it were a putty model; the one who made the change always had the foresight to see what it would look like when settled long years after.

Temples were built, and greenhouses. Roads were closed and new ones made. A canal was dug. Sculptures, walls, rocks, fountains and a cascade have taken their places over four hundred years as if they had grown out of the ground like the flowers and trees which surround them. Light and movement came through waterworks which perhaps no other English garden can match. Forest trees planted at the times of Lancelot Brown and Joseph Paxton have now reached maturity. More are planted every year: together with shrubs and flowers of shorter lives, they are the choice of those in charge now.

There were long years of quiet when the family seldom came here and nothing new was done and there were times of frenzied activity. Some ambitious schemes meticulously carried out were later destroyed – notably London and Wise's parterres and terraces of the 1690s, the seven-acre kitchen garden three-quarters of a mile distant in the park, Paxton's Great Conservatory and his Lily House – and new ones have taken their place.

A garden must change by its very nature. I have tried to describe and illustrate how the garden at Chatsworth came to look as it does now, at the turn of yet another century.

Deborah Devonshire

Chatsworth, 1999

Our garden is an inhibiting place to go out with a trowel. It covers a hundred and five acres and is contained by a wall one and three-quarter miles long, and this in turn is surrounded by a thousand acres of parkland encompassed by nearly ten miles of deer fence.

The outline of the garden is often obscured by trees and shrubs as it wanders in an undisciplined way, sometimes merging with the park as a ha-ha, sometimes as a daunting eight-feet-high dry stone wall. Within this enclosure you can find survivals of the original Elizabethan garden and other easily recognisable features from the last four centuries.

Like the house, the garden is a mongrel product of layer upon layer of history and has changed immeasurably over four hundred and fifty years. Now the different styles merge with each other almost imperceptibly.

The first garden surrounding Bess of Hardwick's house of the 1550s, with a parterre and ponds to the south (*opposite, above,* from a copy by Richard Wilson of a lost painting). The 1st Duke's new house and garden in *c.*1707 with elaborate terraces, fountains, parterres and the Cascade (*opposite, below,* from a painting by an unknown artist in a private collection). The 4th Duke's garden *c.*1760, with the new stables and bridge, but with most of the terraces removed (*right,* from a painting by William Marlow). Today the lay out of the garden is much as the 6th Duke left it in the 1850s (*below*).

'Adorn'd with Embellishments'

Bess of Hardwick, the 1st Earls
and the 1st Duke

1549—1707

Bess of Hardwick, attributed to Rowland Lockey.

Previous pages The South Front. Some genius set the Canal higher than the lawn so the house appears to rise from the water.

The story of the garden is inextricably mixed with the story of the family. It starts in 1555 when Elizabeth Hardwick (*c.* 1527–1608), always known as Bess of Hardwick, and her second husband Sir William Cavendish (1505–57), the progenitors of the Cavendish dynasty in Derbyshire, began to build their house on the Chatsworth land they bought in 1549.

Their garden was much smaller than it is now and differently arranged around the house. There was a formal plot to the south with ponds and fountains – not necessarily where they are today. The steep hill to the east was terraced and a high wall enclosed a roe park where bucks were fattened for the table. Fish ponds were dug between the house and the River Derwent. In one of them stood, and still stands, a square stone tower embellishing what was said to be an ancient earthwork which guarded a ford across the river. It is called Queen Mary's Bower. It got its name in Bess's time when her fourth and last husband, the Earl of Shrewsbury, was appointed by Queen Elizabeth as custodian of Mary, Queen of Scots. The story goes that the royal prisoner was allowed to 'take the air' there as long as Lord Shrewsbury accompanied her. It was then within the garden walls as well as surrounded on three sides by water and it was supposed that rescuers could not reach her. There is no substantiation for this story, but Mary's Bower has always been the subject of romantic legend and is a much loved part of the Chatsworth scenery.

In 1560 Bess ordered *'al kynde of earbes and flowres, and some pece of yt with malos'* to be sown. Roses were planted as well as honeysuckles, irises, pinks and pansies, which are so familiar from the embroideries now to be seen and wondered at in her other great house, Hardwick Hall, only seventeen miles from Chatsworth. Orchards with fruit trees set in patterns, stoutly built stone gazebos, arbours and pavilions completed the Tudor garden.

The massive containing wall running south from the house topped by a balustrade, then the boundary between garden and park, Queen Mary's Bower (restored by Wyatville in the 1830s) and the Hunting, or Stand, Tower (1587) 300 feet up on the cliff to the east are the only visible evidence which remain today of Sir William and Bess, their house and garden.

Above Queen Mary's Bower. The Bower stood in Bess's time, but it was heavily restored in the romantic style in 1823–4. The Hunting, or Stand, Tower is visible on the hill above.

Bess died in 1608. She cordially disliked Henry, her ne'er-do-well elder son, and left all she could to her second and favourite son William Cavendish (1552–1625), who was created Baron Cavendish in 1605 and Earl of Devonshire in 1618. His invaluable contribution to Chatsworth was to commission William Senior to make a survey of his estates. Sixty-five maps, drawn and brightly painted on vellum, dated 1617, are in the library today. Senior's impression of the immediate surroundings of the house is tantalisingly vague, but it shows the extent and layout, in relation to the house, of the garden and park which William's parents had created.

William, 2nd Earl (1590–1628), had only three years in charge of Chatsworth and was succeeded by his son, another William (1617–84). This Lord Cavendish was an intellectual interested in science and literature, and was a founding fellow of the Royal Society in 1663. Although Royalist by inclination, he followed the family motto 'safety through caution' and went abroad during the Civil War, but his younger brother, Charles Cavendish, was killed fighting for the King. Chatsworth was occupied by Royalists and Cromwellians in turn.

Lord Cavendish returned with the peace and the Restoration of the Monarchy and set about improving the house in a haphazard way. The foundations could not support the height of the building and it became unsafe. It was left to his son to finish the job. Meanwhile he began to modernise his garden in earnest. The first mention of a parterre is in 1659. John

Walker, diarist, wrote in 1677 of *'a kind of hanging garden cutt out in Walkes under ye Rockes with Basins, Jettos and Fountains, but as yet unfinished'*.[1]

From 1675 to 1687 there are entries in the accounts for moving and planting lime trees, removing banks of earth and spreading it in the park, *'getting, laying and breaking stone into gravel for walks in ye wilderness'*, making holes for trees and planting them, mixing dung, carrying earth, making banks, making borders and sowing hayseeds and, most significant, *'digging places for fountains and trenches for pipes'* in 1675–6 shortly before Walker's visit. Four men were paid £11 15s. 4d. for *'mowing the best gardens all summer'* and *'several women'* were paid 4d. a day for working 1,282 days *'weeding, planting flowers and such like work'*.

Charles Cotton described the garden in the latter half of the 1670s:

> *'Now in the middle of this great Parterre,*
> *A Fountain darts her streams into the Air*
> *Twenty Foot high ...*
> *Where the Ground swells nearer the Hill above,*
> *And where once stood a Crag and Cherry Grove,*
> *(Which of renown, then shar'd a mighty Part)*
> *Instead of such a barbarous piece of Art,*
> *Such poor contriv'd, dwarfish and ragged shades,*
> *Tis now adorn'd with Fountains and Cascades,*
> *Terrass on Terrass with their Stair-cases*
> *Of brave and great contrivance, and to these*
> *Statues, Walks, Grass-plats, and a Grove indeed,*
> *Where silent lovers may lye down and bleed ...'*

and concludes

> *'That this is Paradise, which seated stands*
> *In midst of Desarts, and of barren Sand.*
> *So a bright Diamond would look, if set*
> *In a vile Socket of ignoble Jet ...'*[2]

It is a tragedy for those who came after that there is no pictorial record of these extravagances.

The 4th Earl of Devonshire (1640–1707) succeeded in 1684. He was created Marquess of Hartington and Duke of Devonshire in 1694 for his role in bringing William of Orange to the English throne in 1688. In 1685 he left London and the court of King James II in somewhat of a hurry. The reason for his departure to Chatsworth was not of his choosing, but for the house and the garden it was fortuitous in the extreme. He met a certain Colonel Colepeper *'in the King's Presence Chamber and receiving from him an insulting look he took him by the nose, led him out of the room and gave him some despising blow with the head of his cane'*.[3] For this impetuous act Devonshire was fined £30,000. Instead of paying the fine, he escaped to Derbyshire, and there began the great work for which those who see it now must be thankful to Colonel Colepeper and his insulting look.

This was the golden age of architecture in England and Devonshire had inherited his great-great-grandmother's passion for building. Over a number of years he rebuilt the Elizabethan house in the classic style and constructed a garden to complement it. The quarrelsome William Talman (1650–1719) was his architect from 1687 until 1696, when they fell out. (For some time Talman also acted as deputy superintendent of the royal gardens at

William Cavendish, the 1st Duke, after Sir Godfrey Kneller.

Above Flora's Temple. Built by the 1st Duke in 1695, it was moved to its present site in 1760, when it first became a shelter for Flora. It was restored in 1993 when the pillars were renewed.

Above The statue of Flora is attributed to the sculptor Cibber. First placed on one of the 1st Duke's parterres, she was moved into the temple that now bears her name in 1760. The 6th Duke 'promoted' her to the French (now Rose) Garden in 1813. We returned her to her Temple after 180 years outside.

Opposite The Sea Horse Fountain on the South Lawn. Triton and the four stone sea horses were carved by Cibber.

a salary of £100 a year.) It is thought that Devonshire himself may have been responsible for the West Front, and in 1704–5 Thomas Archer (1668–1743) designed the North Front.

The Duke was one of the first Englishmen to fall for the extravagant creation of formal gardens already fashionable in France, Italy and Holland. The best-known horticulturists, designers and sculptors of the day were engaged. George London designed the west parterre, which was finished in 1690. London (d. 1714) had travelled in France studying the work of le Nôtre for Louis XIV at Versailles and became Master Gardener to William III. Of London, Stephen Switzer recalled that *'this one person actually saw and gave directions once or twice a year in most of the gentlemen's Gardens in England.'*[4] His contract for designing the ground *'west of ye great parterre'* confirms that it was in existence – perhaps the one mentioned in the accounts for 1659. Four years later London's partner, Henry Wise (1653–1738), joined him to reconstruct the south parterre. They were paid £500 for the work. Wise later became Royal Gardener to Queen Anne and George I. He was employed at Hampton Court for many years and there is a strong similarity between the Privy Garden there that he created for William and Mary (which was restored in 1996) and the Chatsworth parterre. The business-like pair were not only designers but suppliers as well. In the 1690s their nursery garden at Brompton Park, Kensington, held *'a stock of plants so large that they would have been worth £40,000 at a penny a piece.'*[5] Now the ground is closely sown with museums. In the 1690s they sold vast quantities of trees to Chatsworth – limes, hollies, junipers, box, orange trees and myrtles, plus 12,000 hornbeams. Their bills are in the muniment room here.

Devonshire's garden, which extended the classical architecture of the house into the surroundings, brought the formality and symmetry favoured on the continent to Derbyshire for the first time.[6] Rectangular and diagonal intersecting paths of yellow and white gravel were laid, some in false perspective from the house to make them look even longer than they were. In addition to the great parterres to the west and south, Bess's terraces, up the slope to the east, were increased in number and decorated with ponds, fountains, statues, and painted and gilded palisades. Bird houses were built, and a greenhouse. This beauty was moved later to its present site by the 6th Duke. It has the curious embellishment of twelve seventeenth-century busts on the roof that were removed from the courtyard of the house by the 6th Duke and his architect Wyatville in *c.* 1824. A bowling green was laid down in the West Garden with its own grandiose shelter built like a classical temple (later it was moved and is now known as Flora's Temple). Levelling, laying out and planting occupied the ten years from 1687.

A Frenchman, Monsieur Huet (his name was soon anglicised to Hewett, described in the account book as 'the French Minister'), supervised the immense work. He was responsible for carrying out London and Wise's plans till 1696, when another Frenchman, Monsieur Audias, took over the job. They followed the Englishmen's interpretation of the strictly formal style begun by le Nôtre in the 1650s at Versailles. This kind of garden needed decoration to complete the picture. The creators of the outdoor works of art in stone, bronze and iron were chosen by the Duke as the best in their time and their work is held in high esteem three centuries later.

The Danish sculptor Caius Gabriel Cibber (1630–1700) spent from 1688 to 1691 working at Chatsworth. Cibber worked for Talman at Thoresby in Nottinghamshire and for Sir Christopher Wren on St Paul's Cathedral and Hampton Court. In 1693 his talent secured him the post of Sculptor in Ordinary to William III. Some of his master works are still to be seen at Chatsworth. Flora has been in and out of her temple over the years and she has kept art historians busy in changing attributions. The stone horses in the Sea Horse Fountain on

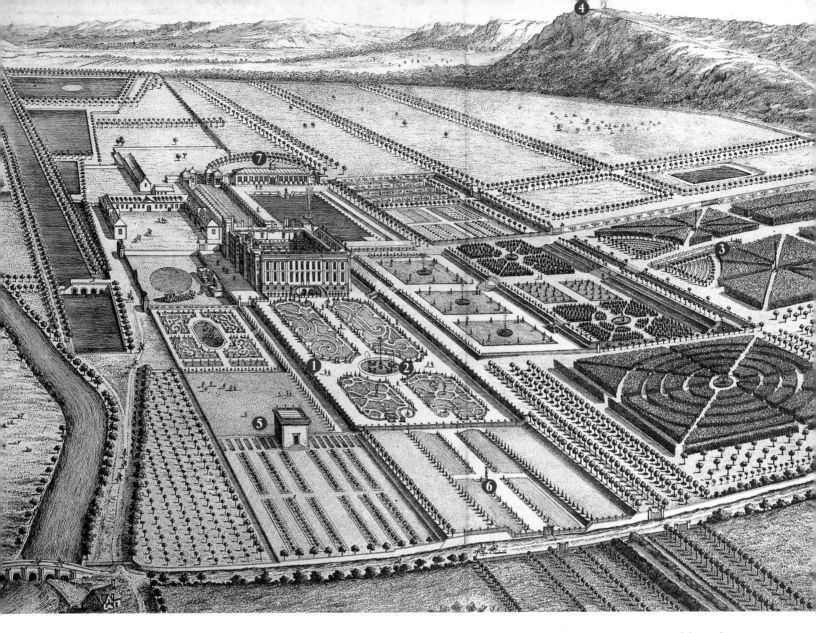

The garden in 1699 from an engraving made by Knyff and Kip. Today they would recognise:

1. The Elizabethan Balustrade
2. The Sea Horse Fountain
3. The Cascade
4. The Hunting Tower;

and also, though they are now in different places:

5. Flora's Temple
6. Flora
7. The 1st Duke's Greenhouse

The Canal (*in the photo opposite*) was dug three years after the engraving was made.

the South Front have been buffeted by three hundred years of spray and have lost some limbs, but they are still full of life and energy. Their heads are covered in yellow lichen and their fat scaly fish tails are coiled over their backs as they prance forever in the confines of their pond. Triton rises from the waters in their midst, blowing his conch shell in the attitude of the captain of the winning team kissing the trophy after the FA Cup Final.

Nature had to be improved upon to delight the Duke and his friends. In 1695 an '*artificial tree of brass*', the ancestor of the present squirting willow tree, was created by one Ibeck. Celia Fiennes wrote, '*about the middle of* [the garden] *by the Grove stands a fine Willow tree, the leaves barke and all looks very naturall, the roote is full of rubbish or great stones to appearance, and all on a sudden by turning a sluce it raines from each leafe but in appearance is exactly like any Willow.*'[7]

Celia's words pour out like '*the spouting water from the pyramids*' she describes. Overwhelmed by the excitement of it all, she rattles on about gravel walks, stone and brass statues and images, basins, squares of grass, a wilderness and shady walks, several fine gardens one without another, close arbours and water from pipes, '*some flush it up that it frothes like snow*'.

We have an engraving made in 1699 by Knyff and Kip recording this transformation scene

(Leendert Knyff was the draughtsman, Jan Kip the engraver) which took so long to complete. The famous pair, who sound like a music hall turn, drew and engraved likenesses of many great houses and gardens in England, and made the surroundings of each one look like Versailles in varying sizes. All are recorded from what seems to have been a seventeenth-century helicopter. Their engraving of Chatsworth shows the shapes of the separate gardens and how they were connected with one another. The individual trees are dots like newly pricked-out annuals, forever frozen in size, never to grow and fudge the outlines and perspectives. It is difficult to believe in their whole vast picture of Chatsworth, but a magnifying glass shows details on the statue of Flora and gives one confidence to accept much of it as a true representation of what they saw three hundred years ago. (Knyff and Kip are to be met all over the world now. Imagine my delight on stepping out of a hotel lift in Los Angeles to find myself face to face with Londesborough[8] in all its glory.)

The steep gradient of the hill to the east of the house had been used to advantage to divert streams creating a supply of water for the fountains and ponds since Bess's day. Now the water was to be harnessed to an even more spectacular effect.

An aerial view of the garden today, taken from the same angle as Knyff and Kip's engraving, which shows the fundamental changes in the garden and park over the last three centuries.

Above Looking east up to the Cascade. Above the Cascade House is the waterfall from the aqueduct in Stand Wood.

Right Restoring the Cascade during the winters of 1995–7. Carl Wragg was the stonemason.

The Cascade

The Cascade was the 1st Duke's masterstroke. Designed by Monsieur Grillet, a French hydraulics engineer with experience in decorative waterworks for Louis XIV and le Nôtre, it took two years to build and was finished in 1696. It is fed by water from a nine-acre reservoir dug under the moor edge high above the house. A series of twenty-four steps and slopes was built in stone, each fall being different so that the sound of the falling water varied. The Duke was for ever changing his mind and only six years later this extraordinary construction was torn up and rebuilt, larger and steeper than before. More than half of it was taken up again in 1826 by the 6th Duke. He described how he found, when he made the wide gravel path that leads up to the Cascade, that *'when the two lines met, an elbow, or long angle, presented itself to the eye'*. Imagine his dismay. Undeterred he replaced them *'true to the lines of the South front, and, consequently, to those of the gravel walk'*. What trouble was taken to get things right. This was not the last time the Cascade was rebuilt.

During the winters of 1995–97 thirty-five tons of new stone from the quarries at nearby Stanton Moor were used to replace the old, which had been worn away by the water over the previous 170 years. All twenty-four slopes were re-laid and on each slope the 'dressing' was different. The stones were finished by hand; Carl Wragg, the mason, using a chisel and mallet to make lines – horizontal, vertical or at an angle. A shed with no mod cons was built for him and he chipped away for months. It was a joy to watch him; no fudging or rubbing out was possible and each finished stone was a work of art.

Thomas Archer, the architect of the North Front of the house, drew the perfect little water temple at its head. It was finally finished with much embellishment in 1711. It is a theatrical building, like others in the garden, where nature has long been subordinated to art in the form of architecture. The Cascade appears to spring from it. Standing inside the building when the water is turned on to run over the roof you feel like an aquatic creature ready to swim with the silvery torrent down the stone stairs.

The water temple was lavishly decorated with frostwork and carvings by Henri Nadauld (1653–1723). A river god lies on his side sound asleep on the roof. A couple of nymphs holding pitchers carelessly spill more water into basins which overflow into the pond feeding the Cascade itself. Two mythical winged creatures, griffins with prominent backbones and ribs, spout out yet more water. Nadauld was a Huguenot refugee who, during the years of religious persecution on the continent when some of the most talented craftsmen of the late seventeenth and early eighteenth centuries came to work in England, joined other refugees on the virtuoso team who did so much to embellish Chatsworth. Samuel Watson (1662–1715) carved the festoons, scrolls and shells and added the four lions heads under the cupola above. A local man, Watson carved equally skilfully in stone, wood and alabaster; his wood carving is often mistaken for that of Grinling Gibbons. He worked in and out of doors at Chatsworth from 1691 to 1711.

Below The 1990s restoration of the Cascade took 10,000 man hours to complete. As much original stone as possible was used.

Above One of the twenty-four series of steps that make the Cascade. Each is different – either in the shape, number or height of the risers – to vary the sound of the falling water.

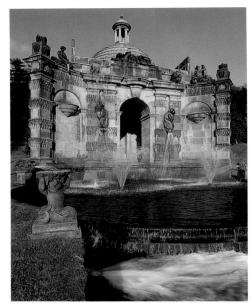

Above and right Water froths over the roof of the Cascade House, and is forced through thirteen spouts, including the mouths of two weighty dolphins precariously hung between the pilasters. It also sprays up through two small jets in the pool in front of the house before tumbling down the steps.

The Canal

The boldest alteration of all was the levelling of *'the great slope'* at the end of the south parterre which *'opened a distant prospect to the blue hills and made on the same level with his house and garden a canal.'*[9] In his tour through Derbyshire in the 1720s Daniel Defoe wrote, *'to make a clear vista or prospect beyond into the flat country, towards Hardwick, another seat of the same owner, the duke, to whom what others thought impossible, was not only made practicable, but easy, removed, and perfectly carried away a great mountain that stood in the way, and which interrupted the prospect'.*[10] The prospect did not reach as far as Hardwick, which is seventeen miles away and in another direction, but it opened the view over the Old Park southwards to give a new spaciousness to the whole.

The canal, 314 yards long and about 2 feet deep with stone sides and a giant 'plug' at the south end which acts as an overflow, has been a vital feature of the garden ever since. A fountain played in the same place as the present-day one – no doubt a consequence of the pipes laid in 1675. Two river gods, attributed to Nadauld, sit on their stone plinths flanking the fountain.

Three hundred years later the Canal gives little trouble and a great deal of pleasure. It must be cleared of twigs and litter and the edges cleaned so that they appear sharp, but on the whole it looks after itself. One of my sons-in-law caught a mass of crayfish from its murky bottom using kippers for bait. He put them alive in their muddy water in the bath next to the best visitor's bedroom, which nearly caused a revolution in our household.

The expenses incurred by work in the garden were small compared to those for the rebuilding of the house, which employed the greatest artists and craftsmen of the day. But the whole enterprise stretched the Duke's purse to the limit and beyond, and like others before him he took to gambling. Racing was his passion and there was always a chance that a successful bet would solve his problems. He may have had impeccable taste, but he was not a good employer, often decamping to Newmarket, where his fortune was closely followed by his steward, Aaron Kinton, when the payment of the army of workers often depended on the outcome of a race or on the turn of a card.

The Canal, seen from the roof of the house on a summer's morning. At the far end is the Frink *War Horse* that looks south over the Old Park. At the near, north, end are the river gods and the rock-surrounded base of the Emperor Fountain. The row of three-hundred-year-old limes stands to the west.

On 20 April 1704 Kinton wrote to Whildon (accountant and receiver) that *'His Grace lost a good sume at Newmarket Last week and is to goe there againe in 10 dayes but must first raise about 2500£ to make stakes, but how this will be I see not, his Grace talkes that he will raise it on the Creditt of Lady-day rents.'* Desperate for cash to pay the wages, he wrote on 5 October, *'... and now I have sent all I have and much more, and not a peny Left and Ld Hartington* [the Duke's son] *angry and a storme of old debts dayly Demanded and what the issue will be god knows, his Grace Lost his Great match on Munday, and wee heare great ods against him yesterday god send better Luck.'* God failed to oblige and poor Kinton went into a decline. But the work went on.

Travellers who went to Chatsworth were unanimous in their delight in the Duke's achievements in bringing an island of civilisation to 'the savage and dreary' surrounding Peak District. Their descriptions of house and garden are lyrical. *'Nothing certainly can be more pleasant than the shady walks on every side, where as from Heaven, one may survey the distant horrors of a*

hellish country,' wrote Joseph Taylor. *'A Noble Palace, adorn'd with all the Embellishments of the most exquisite workmanship; delicate Gardens, beautified with all the Rarityes Curiosity can invent, in the midst of a most barbrous Country.'*[11]

Daniel Defoe agreed. *'Nothing can be more surprising ... than for a stranger coming from the north ... and wandering or labouring to pass this difficult desart country, and seeing no end of it, and almost discouraged and beaten out with the fatigue of it, (just such was our case) on a sudden the guide brings him to this precipice, where he looks down from a frightful height, and a comfortless barren and, as he thought, endless moor, into the most delightful valley, with the most pleasant garden, and most beautiful palace in the world: If contraries illustrate, and the place can admit of any illustration, it must needs add to the splendour of the situation, and to the beauty of the building, and I must say (with which I will close my short observation) if there is any wonder in Chatsworth, it is, that any man who had a genius suitable to so magnificent a design, who could lay out the plan for such a house, and had a fund to support the charge, would build it in such a place where the mountains insult the clouds, intercept the sun, and would threaten, were earthquakes frequent here, to bury the very towns, much more the house, in their ruins.'*[12]

So much for the remarkable house and garden, and for the Peak District and its climate. It was some years before nature and landscape were to be admired in their own right.

One of two river gods that loll on stone beds in the Canal. They are attributed to the sculptor Nadauld. Their plinths are in need of restoration; this will happen soon: the lead pipes will be renewed and water will spurt from them again as planned by the 1st Duke.

'All nature is a garden'

The 2nd, 3rd, 4th and 5th Dukes

1707—1811

Previous pages Looking west over the River Derwent and Paine's Bridge to the park. The view was planned and planted by Lancelot 'Capability' Brown in the 1760s; the five young oaks in the middle distance ought to be removed as they interfere with Brown's original opening to the horizon.

Below William Kent's unexecuted design for a cascade with grottoes and grand temples for the hill at Chatsworth, *c.* 1743. It was a project intended to transform the 1st Duke's formal cascade into the 'rustic' style that Kent had displayed, on a smaller scale, in the grotto at Chiswick House. Kent shows himself explaining his plan to the family.

The 2nd Duke's (1673–1729) interests lay in the arts, not gardens. It was he who bought a collection of Old Master drawings and paintings, coins and antique carved gems to adorn the interior of his London house. His possessions, unusually at that time, were available to be studied by scholars. At Chatsworth he ensured that all was properly maintained, but, apart from planting thousands of trees on the escarpment (which he neglected to fence so they did not survive) and tinkering with the south parterre in 1713, when 7,000 box plants were ordered, he left his father's wonderful garden little changed.

The year before he died, 1728, saw the first glimpse of a change of heart to the simplification of the geometric patterns of the previous generation. The accounts tell us that John Sale and partners were paid for *'levelling, getting turfe and laying it down in ye garden before the South Front'*, and that 135 hedge yews and 'ball yew' were ordered for the south parterre. The fashion for glades and grass was to sweep the country and change the surroundings of most of the great houses to what we know now as the English park. So strong was the desire for change that most of the gardens got the same treatment, Chatsworth not excepted.

The 3rd Duke (1698–1755), Knight of the Garter, sometime MP for Derbyshire and Lord Lieutenant of Ireland 1737–44, was in spite of the foregoing important roles *'plain in his manners and negligent in his dress'*.[13] It was he who promoted a rush of activity and change from the 1730s, when the undoing of the old layout was begun in earnest. There is a bill for *'stubbing up of all the Fir Trees'*, and 2,200 trees were felled.

Earth moving for levelling terraces begun in his father's time was accelerated. He added new and moved existing garden buildings. In 1738 an Ananas House was built and pineapples to fill it were brought from London in 1740. The Bowling Green House (now called Flora's Temple) and the 1st Duke's Greenhouse were pulled down and re-built in their present positions. *'The greenhouse is down'* he wrote to his son, Lord Hartington, in 1749 and the following year *'they are at work ... and will soon have done.'* The wall with its screen of simple iron railings containing the West Garden was demolished in 1752, leaving the carved stone pedestals surmounted by Cibber's sphinxes in isolation. The ground between the house and the river became a lawn down to the water.

As we have seen, the Duke had a sure instinct in matters of taste when a major step had to be taken. Devonshire House in Piccadilly was burnt down in 1733 and it was William Kent (?1685–1748) who was commissioned to rebuild it, design the furniture and decorate the main rooms. So this versatile genius was already well known to the Duke when in about 1743 he drew designs for possible alterations to the Cascade and some fanciful buildings on the hillside above. These were not carried out, but there is no doubt Kent's influence at Chatsworth was strong. He was one of the leaders of the new style of gardening and we are often reminded that it was Kent who *'leapt the fence and saw all nature was a garden'*.[14]

A closer link with Kent was through Richard, 3rd Earl of Burlington (1694–1753), father-in-law of the 4th Duke, himself an architect, follower of Palladio and the most influential man of taste of his time. He was the friend and patron of Kent, and together they were responsible for many of the artistic achievements of the first half of the eighteenth century, including the 'naturalisation' of gardens. It was to Burlington that Alexander Pope, poet, wit and man of letters, addressed his epistle on taste: *'tired of the scenes parterres and fountains yield he finds at last he better likes a field'*.[15] Lord Burlington's only surviving daughter, Lady Charlotte Boyle (1731–54), married the 3rd Duke's son, Lord Hartington, in 1748. Charlotte, the richest heiress in England, died of smallpox in 1754 when she was only twenty-three, before her husband succeeded. She left four children, the eldest of whom became the 5th Duke and through his mother inherited all Lord Burlington's properties and works of art, including an incomparable architectural library.

The 3rd Duke died in 1755 and the following year only routine items like mole killing and ditching were carried out. It was a lull before the storm. By this time the attitude to gardens in this country was undergoing a profound change.

Fashion is like a breeze which goes through the air almost imperceptibly at first, gathering strength as those with influence decide on something new, whether it is clothes, children's names, painting, architecture or gardening. So the word spread and the old order changed. Although Kent's suggestions for Chatsworth were not carried out, they showed the way the wind was blowing, and a few years later it fell to the 4th Duke to finish the job of destroying what was left of his great-grandfather's creation.

The 4th Duke — MP for Derbyshire,[16] Lord Treasurer and then Lord Lieutenant and Governor General of Ireland, Prime Minister 1756–7, Knight of the Garter and Lord Chamberlain of the Household till 1762 — had only nine years to carry out still more improvements to his Chatsworth estate in the new style.

In about 1760 he engaged that much-travelled landscape man Lancelot 'Capability' Brown (1716–83) to bring the 'romantic' movement to Chatsworth. Destructive as he was in the garden, Brown was peerless as a designer of parks. He was far too busy dashing round the country at the behest of every landowner worth his salt, changing the surroundings of all the big houses you have ever heard of, to spend a long time at Chatsworth and he delegated the work to his foreman, Milliken.

The Duke's men carried out the work at speed. With the new enthusiasm for the 'natural', when straight lines were abominated, it was a miracle that the Cascade and the Canal were spared. Had the ultra-fashionable had their way, those too would have gone, but it is the strength of the place that there is room for features from all ages and styles, both in and out of doors. Knyff and Kip hovering above the house would have spotted these, and they would have been surprised to see that the Bowling Green House and the Greenhouse had been moved, but they would have seen little else to remind them of what they had recorded in such detail sixty-five years earlier.

Horace Walpole underlined the change of heart when he enthused about the landscape and criticised nearly everything else. The condemnation of the hateful surroundings by travellers of two generations earlier were turned upside down and raw nature took over as the ideal. In 1760, in a letter to George Montagu, he wrote, *'I was never more disappointed than at Chatsworth, which, ever since I was born, I have condemned. It is a glorious situation; the vale rich in corn and verdure, vast woods hang down the hills, which are green to the top, and the immense rocks only serve to dignify the prospect. The river runs before the door, and serpentises more than you can conceive in the vale. The Duke is widening it, and will make it the middle of his park; but I don't approve an idea they are going to execute, of a fine bridge with statues under a noble cliff. If they will have a bridge (which by the way will crowd the scene), it should be composed of rude fragments, such as the giant of the Peak would step upon, that he might not be wet-shod. The expense of the works now carrying on will amount to forty thousand pounds. ... The great jet d'eau I like, nor would I remove it; whatever is magnificent of the kind in the time it was done, I would retain, else all gardens and houses wear a tiresome resemblance. I except that absurdity of a cascade tumbling down marble steps, which reduces the steps to be of no use at all.'*[17]

William Cavendish, the 4th Duke, by Thomas Hudson.

Naturalising the surroundings

Eight years after the revolutionary changes in the landscape had taken place Walpole returned and changed his mind. '*It is much improved by the late Duke, many foolish waterworks being taken away, oaks and rocks taken into the garden, and a magnificent bridge built.*'[18] Magnificent the bridge certainly is. James Paine (*c.* 1716–89) was its architect in the 1760s and he was also responsible for the equally magnificent stables up the hill to the east. The scale of the bridge is just right in its landscape and there is a touch of genius in the angle at which it is set. It stands out when seen from our windows in the morning light, and from it the gilded window frames on the West Front of the house can be gazed upon at sunset. In the wildest winter weather and the hottest summer night I see people there leaning on the parapet drinking in the unrivalled beauty of the view.

Flowers were banished out of sight when deer and sheep were let in to graze what had once been the meticulously kept patterned garden described by Horace Walpole as '*the mechanic taste of the Dutch*'. To complete the 'improvements' a quantity of trees and shrubs and a few perennial plants were imported in 1759 from Philadelphia USA, including pines, cedars, catalpa, sassafras, hickory, euonymus, witch hazel and maples. I would love to know if any survived the journey.

An immense programme of afforestation was put in hand further afield. Vast quantities of acorns were planted, together with other native hardwood trees. Among such major expenses noted in the accounts we are brought down to earth with the entry for 27 August 1760: '*pots of treacle to catch ye wasps when at ye fruit 2/-*'.

All but three of the fountains (those in the Ring Pond, the Canal and the Sea Horse Fountain) were thrown out and their ponds filled in. Topiary and avenues disappeared, the smoothed terraces degenerated into tree-to-tree carpets of grass, a ha-ha was constructed to trick the eye into thinking the garden and the park were one and the same, and forest trees were planted in apparently natural clumps in both park and garden so there was no demarcation between the two.

How they must have revelled in the idyllic scenery they had to work on, with dramatic elements provided by the rocky escarpment to the east giving a backdrop like that in a theatre '*so covered with a wood of beautiful trees, that you see no hill, only a rising wood, as if the trees grew so much higher than one another, and was only a wall of trees, whose tops join into one another so close, as nothing is seen through them.*'[19] The river in the valley below and the rolling hills to the west were ready to be enclosed and planted to make a vast pleasure ground.

In all England, the admirers of the picturesque could not have found a better stage on which to work than that at Chatsworth. The essential ingredients were theirs in abundance – hills, rocks, streams, waterfalls, ponds, ancient oaks, a river and even a precipice were provided by nature to be moulded to the new ideal. In other parks small streams were dammed to make pretend rivers as an excuse to build a bridge to complete the scene. Here a bridge was not an ornament but a necessity spanning a real river. The grand stage set of scenery to show off the noble house was complete.

Above The West Front of the house with Paine's Bridge in the foreground. Every day of the year, whatever the weather, I see people standing on the bridge gazing at this incomparable view of the house, planned by the 4th Duke and his architect, James Paine. The trees on the steep hill behind the house now make a perfect background.

Opposite The bridge seen from the south-east. Paine embellished the bridge with statues, probably by Cibber, which date from the time of the 1st Duke.

Above The wide expanse of the Salisbury lawns that, sadly, replaced the 1st Duke's series of terraces to the east of the house. The North Wing with the theatre topped by a belvedere was built in the 1820s by the 6th Duke. Since this photograph was taken, the sixteen urns that crowned the belvedere's four turrets, and which were removed during the 1920s, have been copied and replaced.

The Salisburys

This prairie of a lawn is called the Salisburys, after the Plain, I suppose, and is divided by a broad gravel path in line with the Cascade into two parts, Great and Little. The Great Salisbury covers just under three acres and the Little, up to the beech hedge, just over two and a half, giving 5.57 acres in total.

The Salisburys is the site of the old terraces, each with its fountain surrounded by patterns of box or yew and the small clipped trees so clearly shown in the Knyff and Kip engraving on page 16. The terraces broke up the steep slope on the eastern approach of the house in what must have been an ideal way.

Earth moving on a large scale had been going on for some years and in the 1760s the 'naturalisation' (or the destruction, if that is how you see it) of the garden was completed. The preparation for the new lawns took four years. Between April 1762 and October 1766 the accounts tell us: *'Ploughing ... to lay it down to grass seed £1.14s.'*, *'For 20 quarters of hay seeds at Sheffield to sow the new laid down grounds £8'*, and *'Rolling and harrowing the new ground £3'.*

It was here that the change from formality was most evident. The result was summed up in 1949 by Francis Thompson, the librarian here for many years. *'What has often been remarked as the only defect in the situation of Chatsworth — a want of depth and spaciousness in its background — the slope rising from the very foot of the building has the effect of seeming to push it forward into the river.'*[20]

Several times I have been stopped by strangers walking here on these featureless sweeps

of mown grass who ask, 'Excuse me, but can you tell me where the garden is?' Disappointing, and all Brown's fault.

We may weep over the loss of the terraces, but there are compensations. The panoramic view from the Salisburys to the west is a delight which never palls and we can only rejoice in the 4th Duke's and Brown's work, through his foreman Milliken, in creating one of the most beautiful parks in England. I am always thankful that Brown did not persuade his patron to dam the river in front of the house to make one of those soggy lakes which were his trademark. Instead he and the Duke planted the distant contours on a huge scale which gives the house and garden the frame it deserves and accentuates the perfect position of the building in its landscape. Along the far hills the wedge-shaped planting ensures a continuous outline of trees – when one segment is cut down another is high enough to take its place. Although it is only a narrow plantation it succeeds in making you imagine it to be a boundless forest. A mill and cottages on the 'flat' across the river were razed, new roads and gates were made and the park took on the appearance it has today.

The 'grass' on the Salisburys is not what it seems, but is made up of an abundance of wild flowers of the kind abhorred by anyone who prefers a lawn to consist of a single species of bright green grass with no variation in colour or texture. After rain, slippery patches covered in a slimy algae appear. Best clothes have been ruined by falls here. In 1982 we thought of smartening it up and called in the Sports Turf Research Institute to advise on treatment. As

Above Looking west across the Park to the circle of beech trees and New Piece Wood beyond. The wedge-shaped blocks of trees along the contour were planned by Brown to enclose the Park. They have been felled and replanted many times since in order to maintain the afforested skyline that Brown envisaged.

Overleaf Looking over the Salisburys and the Broad Walk. On one side the Walk is lined with Irish yews that are clipped and bound, and on the other with those left to grow naturally.

31

luck would have it, at the same time, Dr O. L. Gilbert, lecturer in the department of Landscape Architecture at Sheffield University, wrote a piece on these lawns describing the species growing there.[21] He listed ladies' smock, mantle and bedstraw, dog violet, yarrow, knapweed, ox-eye daisy, mouse-eared hawk weed, cat's ear, bird's-foot trefoil, tormentil, harebell, milkwort, field woodrush, heath bedstraw, selfheal, sorrel, speedwell, white clover and even yellow mountain pansy, as well as sedges, fifteen different mosses in the wet places, plus large patches of heather and the common lawn plants – dandelion, creeping buttercup, plantain and daisy.

The first application of lime had already been applied when Dr Gilbert's article was published, but the recommended repeated doses of fertiliser had not. In the light of his findings the planned 'improvements' were immediately stopped and the single application of lime had no lasting effect. Laid down and sown nearly two hundred and fifty years ago and continuously grazed or mown, except in wartime, ever since, it is probably the last survivor of such a lawn. I sometimes wonder if the people who picnic and play games and the children who roll down the steepest slopes know what is underfoot.

There were several big beeches between the Rose Garden and the Cascade and more on the rough grass before you reach the Ring Pond, planted presumably at the time the lawn was laid down. Like most of Brown's beeches, they had reached the end of their lives and we reluctantly cut them down in 1993. Two remain, but I am afraid they show signs of decay and their days are numbered.

Although the 4th Duke had only nine years in charge at Chatsworth his fundamental changes left the garden and park much as they appear today. After his death in 1764 there followed almost half a century of inactivity.

Not only did the 5th Duke (1748–1811) prefer London to the country and seldom stay long at Chatsworth, but he was a profoundly idle man who did not bother to make changes. At the age of sixteen he succeeded his father as *'a torpid minor; and torpid he continued to be throughout life'.*[22] However, he did allow work to be done in the house, and bought some 'Frenchified' furniture – most likely at the instigation of his charming and more energetic wife, born Lady Georgiana Spencer. The lack of interest in the garden was reflected in the fact that the total of the gardeners' wages amounted to £100 a year, representing perhaps seven men. The only addition was the Grotto built for Georgiana in 1798.

Below The Grotto built for Georgiana in 1798. The dottily out-of-place bandstand was added by her son, the 6th Duke.

The Grotto

Georgiana was an enthusiastic collector of minerals and White Watson, a local geologist (and grandson of the sculptor Samuel Watson), was her mentor. He was paid '£66-18-9 [out of a total cost of £140-8-3] *for his time and trouble in designing and superintending the making of the Grotto and for fossils'.* It was lined with stalactites and stalagmites and other subterranean finds which abound in the Derbyshire limestone caves. Some

years after Georgiana's death, her son, the 6th Duke, enlarged it by excavating a cave behind it. 'The grotto', he wrote, 'was built by my Mother; and I respected its exterior when the addition was made of a natural cavern, formed of crystals of copper ore that were discovered in Ecton mine, on the borders of Staffordshire, and had to be removed in the hope of finding some of the lost side veins. Vain hope! the produce ceased to repay the labours of the works, instead of amounting, as it is said to have done in one year, to the sum of £300,000 — a fortunate God-send, that paid for the building of Buxton Crescent, and I should hope for a great deal besides. The crystals are curious, because they contain the ore, instead of being, as it usual, encrusted by it.' Little wonder that a night-watchman was appointed to 'guard against depredations'. The Duke also added a bandstand on the roof. It is high time someone engaged a band to play there.

If any living thing could be made permanent in the garden I would choose the row of small-leaved limes (*Tilia cordata*) to the west of the Canal. Dr Johnson *'discoursed under their shade'* after dining here in the summer of 1784 and so, of course, this side of the Canal is called after the irascible old fellow, Dr Johnson's Walk. Georgiana Devonshire wrote to her mother, Lady Spencer, on 7–10 September 1784, *'We did not come down till late and at about one Dr Johnson arriv'd — he look'd ill but they say is wonderfully recover'd. He was in great good humour and vastly entertaining though his first debut was dry — he said upon young Burke asking him if he was quite well — Sir I am not half well, no, nor a quarter well ... but when he got more at his ease the Duke took him under the Lime trees and he was wonderfully agreeable indeed ... Lady Eliz[23] and me were very sorry to leave him for the public day — he din'd here and does not shine quite so much in eating as in conversing, for he eat much and nastily.'[24]*

Fifteen young trees are clearly shown in a painting of 1743, so presumably they were planted when the Canal was dug in about 1702. Eleven of these three-hundred-year-old giants remain. They were planted 21 feet apart and pollarded at about 12 feet high. Each one has four or five big branches which spring from this point and soar up to a height of 118 feet. As the trees are so close together the branches had no chance of growing north and south, but have made up for it by an immense canopy over the ground to the east and west. The biggest spreads 106 feet, nearly reaching the Canal to the east and covering the Green Drive to the west. Perhaps it was because of this unusual angle of growth that the limes withstood the westerly storm of 1962 when hundreds of trees in the park and garden were blown down; in their exposed position they received the full force of the blast, but they all survived.

Above A view of Chatsworth in 1743 by Thomas Smith of Derby showing the 1st Duke's stables and bridge. Eleven of the original fifteen lime trees seen here are still going strong.

Below The row of limes today.

'Bit by Gardening'

The early years of the 6th Duke

1811—1835

The 6th 'Bachelor' Duke, aged twenty-one, by Sir Thomas Lawrence.

On the death of his father in 1811, William Spencer Cavendish, the 6th Duke of Devonshire (always known as the Bachelor Duke), was twenty-one. His upbringing at Devonshire House among legitimate and illegitimate siblings, his mother in a constant state of worry over her gambling debts and his morose, silent father was unusual to say the least. He inherited much of Georgiana's charm and that characteristic shines through his writing in his letters and diaries and in his *Handbook of Chatsworth and Hardwick* (privately printed in 1844). His devotion to Chatsworth and pleasure in his garden were the abiding loves of his life.

He was a collector: rich, extravagant and liberal in his desire to share his good fortune and the enjoyment of his possessions with any passer-by, appreciative of his talented employees, hospitable, a famous host, and at the same time, lonely. He suffered a lengthy attack of religious mania in middle age and had recurring bouts of depression and partly imagined illnesses. In spite of these difficulties his ever-present sense of humour and of the ridiculous endeared him to family and friends. Totally without snobbishness, he was the same with the King or the stable boy, the Queen or the youngest housemaid.

Unusually for a Cavendish, he was not attracted by politics, except when championing the underdog. His humour, sensitivity and charm are preserved in his writings, and his influence at Chatsworth is there for all to see today. You cannot go far, in or out of doors, without feeling his benign presence. The Bachelor Duke was to make the garden world famous once more and the centre of as much attention as it had been in his great-great-great-grandfather's day.

This was the man who inherited not only the old Cavendish estates of Chatsworth and Hardwick Hall in Derbyshire and Devonshire House in London but also, through his grandmother, Charlotte Boyle, all the Burlington possessions as well – Bolton Abbey and Londesborough in Yorkshire, Lismore Castle in County Waterford, and Burlington House and Chiswick House in London, as well as Compton Place at Eastbourne, which had come into the family through marriage in 1782. All these and 200,000 acres of land were now his responsibility.

Previous pages Two of the eight 'stone baskets' in the West Garden built by Wyatville for the 6th Duke in the 1820s. The original golden yew 'cushions' fill the corners, and we have added the sharply clipped box and a central dark green yew. 'New Dawn' and 'Zéphirine Drouhin' roses clamber over the balustrade in the foreground.

Chatsworth was always the family's main country house and so it has remained. The Bachelor Duke inherited a garden which had been sadly neglected by his father. It was an unkempt wilderness and no one had even bothered to clear away growths of self-sown trees and shrubs round the house, which made a fine place for the cooks to throw out their rubbish. *'An impervious wood,'* the Duke called it.

The rebirth on a grand scale was not immediate. Fifteen years were to pass before Joseph Paxton was engaged as head gardener, but a hint of interest in the garden and a return to formality began as soon as 1812 when *'the parterre in front of the greenhouse'* (known later as the French Garden and now the Rose Garden) was laid out. Sixteen years later the columns which had supported the galleries round the inner courtyard of the house were introduced to outline the new parterre. By 1820 he had planted 1,981,065 forest trees on his Derbyshire estate, for which he was awarded the Gold Medal of the Society for the Encouragement of Arts Manufacturers and Commerce.

When Jeffry Wyatt, later Sir Jeffry Wyatville (1766–1840), was appointed architect to the Duke in 1818, more changes took place and building was soon to become his patron's passion. Sir Jeffry was one of the tribe of Wyatts which, in a hundred and fifty years from the middle of the eighteenth century, produced twenty architects and many painters, sculptors and carvers. Jeffry's uncle, Samuel, designed the incomparable farm buildings at Holkham of which I am deeply jealous. On the recommendation of the Bachelor Duke, Jeffry got the commission from George IV for the remodelling of Windsor Castle (1824–40), which sealed his reputation and made his fortune.

The young Duke and his architect set to work, knocking down the old 'offices' to replace them with the immense North Wing, which grew in scale as the building progressed, culminating in the theatre topped by the belvedere as a final flourish.

The Orangery was commissioned from Wyatville by the Duke in 1827 when he was first, as he said, 'bit by gardening'. Paxton had arrived the year before and advised on its construction. There the Duke grew plants that needed protection from the harsh climate of Derbyshire. They gave their owner and all who saw them the greatest joy. '*Among the orange trees here, four came from the Empress Josephine's collection at Malmaison. I believe they are the only survivors, for Lord Ailsa's and Lord Ailesbury's died, and Lord Londonderry's were burnt. The Rhododendron Arboreum was one of those that first astonished the world at Knight's Nursery garden in the King's Road: I was obliged to give £50 in order to possess it here. The poor tree now looks consumptive and worn-out, from having been allowed to flower beyond its strength.* [The R. arboreum in the garden at Lismore is like an enormous mound. With his usual generosity the Duke gave his Irish neighbours cuttings of the thrilling newcomer and it is still to be seen in most of the demesnes up and down the River Blackwater.] *The Altingia Excelsa* [a south-east-Asian timber tree] *was the first I obtained: it was a rare plant when I gave Low, of Clapton, a sum for it nearly as large as the Rhododendron price. On arriving it was put into the Berlin granite tazza, which then stood in the middle of this Orangery: it has been a traveller in its youth, and somehow returned from Petersburg, and was exchanged with Lowe for other plants. The admiration for these plants has since caused their introduction in great numbers.'*

The Berlin granite tazza is now outside the Orangery. It and the Bartolini Vase (still in the

Below, left The house as it was when the 6th Duke inherited it, with what he described as the 'impervious wood' growing beside the East Front (watercolour by Buckler, 1812).

Below, right The view to Flora's Temple looking north along the Broad Walk. During the 1820s the 6th Duke re-faced the East Front, and also added the North Wing and the Broad Walk that runs along it.

Orangery) are just two examples of the Duke's passion for stone, so evident in the house and garden. *'Bartolini copied the Medici Vase for me with great care. At first it was in the Gallery, then was ordered to the pleasure-ground, when I fell to bedecking that region with white marble; but, being wheeled thus far on its way, the effect was so beautiful under orange and araucaria, that it stopped short, and here remains. Of a night it holds powerful lamps, that send up such a magical light on the branches of the Altingia, that people cry out Fairy land.'*

There are two pairs of borders facing each other as you step into the garden via the Orangery or through Flora's Temple. One pair is planted with blue and white flowers and the other in yellows, oranges and reds. It was the latter which made Cecil Beaton throw up his hands and exclaim that it was awful, just 'a retina irritant' and how could I have thought of such a horror. Yet people stop and stare and photograph it in all seriousness, so who is right? What is taste but your own preference? Perhaps one day Virginia creeper, gladioli, lobelia, ageratum, marigolds, and even golden rod and monkey puzzles will be ordered by grand garden designers. Just now they are taboo.

Opposite The blue and white borders outside the Orangery. The planting includes standard 'Iceberg' roses, *Lilium regale*, *Campanula lactiflora* and *Delphinium* Black Knight Group.

Below The Orangery (*left*) much as it was in the 6th Duke's time, with the Bartolini Vase in the centre; and a detail from the Vase (*right, below*) that still stands there. The Berlin tazza (*right, above*) was an acquisition of the 6th Duke's.

Above, from left Plants that grow in the orange borders: *Lobelia* 'Queen Victoria', *Rosa* 'Evelyn Fison', *Crocosmia* × *crocosmiiflora* 'Emily McKenzie'.

Whether you like it or hate it, the 'retina irritant' makes its scorchingly bright mark from June till October. *Crocosmia* × *crocosmiiflora* 'Emily McKenzie', *Rudbeckia* 'Goldquelle', *Rosa* 'Mountbatten' and 'Evelyn Fison', dahlias, hemerocallis, nasturtiums and marigolds let themselves go here. They are backed by a hedge of *Quercus rubra*, an oak with immense leaves coloured all the reds imaginable in the autumn on shoots 6 feet long, which are cut back to their knobbly trunks every year.

Cecil was not offended by the blue and white borders. The *Anchusa azurea* 'Feltham Pride' of intense blue, the softer blue *Campanula pyramidalis*, galtonias for late summer, dear old love-in-a-mist, *Nemophila* (baby blue eyes), glorious crumpled-petalled romneya, violas, delphiniums of course, *Lilium regale* 'Album' to impress and the fascinating celmisia, a present from Waddesdon Manor, Buckinghamshire, are mixed up here.

The Broad Walk

At the same time that the North Wing was being built, Wyatville made the Broad Walk, which runs from Flora's Temple to Blanche's Vase – a distance, in racing terms, of three furlongs or 660 yards. The Bachelor Duke described it. *'Sir Jeffry Wyatville's first great hit out of doors was the invention of the broad gravel walk that is of so much use and ornament here. Observe the row of fine trees of Araucaria imbricata by its side, the vases of Elvdalen porphyry, the profusion of flowers, and a marble vase from Holland that surmounts the steps.'* The porphyry vases are there and so is the marble one, but the *Araucaria* have gone. Imagine the arguments there would be now, not only in the family but with the Authorities, as to whether these monkey puzzles should stay or be cut down.

Now the Broad Walk is bordered by Irish yews, green and golden; those on the house side are clipped and bound and their opposite numbers grow naturally. They are a lesson in the effect of wind on plants. When you reach the south end of the house and lose the shelter it gives from the west, the yews are much smaller than their brothers. Charles de Noailles, that French guru of garden taste to whom all deferred in the years soon after the Second World War when attention was paid to beauty once more, said to me, 'Never cut the top off an Irish yew. It makes it look like a bottle.' We have heeded his advice.

The grass edging is protected by home-made, home-grown bamboo hoops. The stems are cut into uniform lengths, bent, stuck in the turf and fastened with tarred string. Lemon

Opposite The orange borders early in the season (*above*). Later in the season come solidago, helinium and African marigolds (*below left*); and *Crocosmia paniculata* and the flowers of bronze fennel (*below right*).

Above The Broad Walk that runs along the East Front of the house is bordered on one side by a hedge of 'Hidcote' lavender enclosing 'Iceberg' roses and clipped golden yew.

Left The Lion Steps that lead down to the South Front from the Broad Walk are named after the copies of the Medici lions placed here by the 6th Duke in the 1820s. *Verbascum bombyciferum* seeds itself freely on the steps which are bordered by a hedge of golden yew.

trees in pots are wheeled out in June to flank the steps. The climate is not the only reason for their poor attempts at fruiting as the little lemons are pinched by people wondering if they are real.

In the lavender hedge running along the house side of the Broad Walk towards Blanche's Vase there is a discreet memorial to a man who made an indelible impact on Chatsworth: '*A nôtre fils et frère Jean-Pierre Bien Aimé 10 Août 1956–13 Octobre 1996*'.[25] Jean-Pierre Béraud was a chef by profession. During the eighteen years he worked at Chatsworth he blossomed into an inspired manager first of the Farm Shop, which he rescued from bankruptcy, then the restaurant, which caters for 400,000 visitors each season. His death in a car accident at the age of forty will always be deeply regretted by those who knew him. I believe he had a premonition that he would die young. He told Diane, his wife, laughingly then, that his ashes were to be scattered near the windows of our kitchen where he had reigned with such brilliance and authority. When the sad time came his wishes were carried out.

The length of the Broad Walk is flanked by statues. The Duke described his purchases from Italy: '*Eight statues and two vases have been worked for me by Francesco Bienaime at Carrara, of hard marble of that place, that appears to defy the climate of the Peak, and to resist all incipient vegetation on its surface. I think them a great addition; the eye reposes with pleasure on those classic forms.*'

I think they look a little out of place on their local sandstone plinths and the marble has not resisted the incipient vegetation: the surfaces are grey with various growths. Perhaps this is an improvement, as they might have been too starey white if they had not begun to mature a little to blend with the grey-green northern landscape.

The Lion Steps from the Broad Walk to the South Front and the slope which runs north and south of them replaced a high retaining wall. The Duke wrote: '*From below it was unsightly, from above so imperceptible that a race down the hill is talked of between Charles Fox and Lord John Townshend in which the former, unconscious of the wall, yet unable to stop in time, came down and broke his leg.*' Imagine the fuss there would be now if two important politicians were fooling about and one broke his leg falling over an unfenced drop. The Health and Safety Officer would get out some forms and everyone would be arrested.

The steps are named after the pair of 'Medici' lions that the Duke put there; now they are borderd by a yew hedge. There is a single string with a 'PRIVATE' notice at the top. In all the years I have lived here I remember only three or four occasions when anyone crossed it.

The view up the Broad Walk reminds me of the elm avenue up a slope at Hidcote Manor, Gloucestershire, which led, apparently, to heaven. It was a casualty of elm disease, that calamity which changed the look of rural England (and Hyde Park) irrevocably in the 1970s. Luckily our trees are beeches. As you make for the sky at the high point of the path you reach the enormous vase made of local sandstone with the single word 'BLANCHE' cut into it. It is the Bachelor Duke's memorial to his adored niece, born Blanche Howard,[26] who married his heir William Cavendish, Earl of Burlington. Her death in 1840, at the age of twenty-eight, was a tragedy from which her husband never recovered. Her uncle loved her deeply. '*There are many things at Chatsworth that I should not have allowed myself to do had I not reposed in the thoughts of being succeeded by a person so indulgent, so much attached to me as Blanche.*'

When seen from Flora's Temple the avenue makes a good arch over Blanche's Vase, but when you reach it you see the dismal result of indecision where an avenue is concerned: some of the beeches are old, some middle-aged and some new – a meaningless combination which does not answer. A clean sweep is what is needed, but I haven't got the courage – or the energy, as it would cause endless controversy – to cut it down and plant again.

Above An early nineteenth-century English marble figure, after the so-called Nemesis in the Vatican. It is one of the statues on the Broad Walk bought by the 6th Duke.

Overleaf The view to Blanche's Vase along the Broad Walk and up the beech avenue.

Below Blanche's Vase, commissioned by the 6th Duke.

Joseph Paxton by Henry Briggs.

Joseph Paxton

The advent of Joseph Paxton was as important for the appearance of the surroundings of Chatsworth as that of Wyatville was for the house itself.

Paxton was born in 1803 according to the Duke (but in 1801 acccording to Paxton himself), at Milton Bryant near Woburn Abbey in Bedfordshire, the youngest of a large family of farmers and gardeners. After several jobs near his home he was accepted as a student by the Royal Horticultural Society in 1823 and worked on the ground rented by the Society from the Duke of Devonshire which adjoined the garden of Chiswick House. The Duke sometimes went through a door in the wall to walk in the neighbouring garden, where he talked to the young man in charge of newly introduced plants. Years later he wrote this account of how the twenty-three-year-old Paxton came to work for him, prefacing it with an appreciation of the gardener who became his valued friend.

'Here, supposing that you are looking at all things with new eyes, you will first perceive, in the health and arrangement of the plants, traces of the management and skill attached to a name that will be for ever connected with Chatsworth, the name of one who has multiplied every attraction it possessed. The creations of his talent are remarkable and conspicuous whichever way you turn. The good sense, benevolence, and simplicity of his character dispose all people well towards him. His boundless enthusiasm for the beautiful and marvellous in nature, controlled by a judgement that is faultless in execution, and a taste that is as refined as it is enterprising and daring, are the cause of increased approbation in those who observe in his habits and character the most practical, the most zealous, and the least obtrusive of servants. Exciting the good will and praise of the highest and the lowest, unspoiled and unaltered, he has risen to something like command over all persons who approach him, without one instance of a complaint, or a word said or insinuated against him by anybody, to me, or to any other person. Beloved and blessed by the poor, considered and respected by all. To me a friend, if ever man had one.

'The young man had made a large lake in 1822 at Sir Gregory Page Turner's place near Woburn. He came to Chatsworth in 1826. You shall have it in his own words. "I left London by the Comet coach for Chesterfield, arrived at Chatsworth at half past four o'clock in the morning of the ninth of May, 1826. As no person was to be seen at that early hour, I got over the greenhouse gate by the old covered way, explored the pleasure-grounds, and looked round the outside of the house. I then went down to the kitchen-gardens, scaled the outside wall, and saw the whole of the place, set the men to work there at six o'clock; then returned to Chatsworth and got Thomas Weldon to play me the water-works, and afterwards went to breakfast with poor dear Mrs Gregory and her niece: the latter fell in love with me, and I with her, and thus completed my first morning's work at Chatsworth before nine o'clock." '

Paxton did indeed marry the niece, Sarah Bown, only months later, in 1827. Sarah was a great character in her own right and during her husband's long absences abroad when travelling with the Duke she made sure that work continued as he had planned and kept him up to date with all that was going on at home with endless correspondence.

The Duke and everyone at Chatsworth immediately recognised the new gardener's talents and his ability to motivate the men as never before.

'In a very short time a great change appeared in pleasure-ground and garden: vegetables, of which there had been none, fruit in perfection, and flowers. The twelve men with brooms in their hands on the lawn began to sweep, the labourers to work with activity. The kitchen-garden |the old one, at Barbrook| was so low, and exposed to floods from the river, that I supposed the first wish of the new gardener would be to remove it to some other place – but he made it answer. In 1829 the management of the woods was entrusted to him, and gradually they were rescued from a prospect of destruction. Not till 1832 did I take to caring for my plants in earnest. The old greenhouse was converted into a stove, the greenhouse at the gardens was built, the Arboretum invented and formed. Then started up Orchidacae, and three successive houses were built to receive their increasing numbers. In 1835 the intelligent gardener, John Gibson, was despatched to India to secure the Amherstia nobilis, and other treasures of the East. The colossal new Conservatory was invented and begun in 1836; the following year Baron Ludwig was so charmed with its conception, that he stripped his garden at the Cape of the rarest produce of Africa. Paxton has now been employed in the superintendence and formation of my roads; he had made one tour with me in the West of England, and in 1838 contrived to accompany me for an entire year abroad, in which time, having gone through Switzerland and Italy, he trod in Greece, Turkey, Asia Minor, Malta, Spain and Portugal. In absence he managed that no progress should be checked at home: a great calamity ruined the expedition he had set on foot to California; the unfortunate Wallace and Banks, young gardeners from Chatsworth, having been drowned in Columbia river. He went with me in 1840 to Lismore – and in that year the Conservatory was finished. The village of Edensor was new-modelled, and rebuilt, between 1839 and 1841, and now the crowning works have been the fountains and the rock garden.'

The head gardener's wages in 1826 were £70 a year plus a cottage.

It was Chatsworth's good fortune that in the years of Paxton's reign over the garden it was the Duke and Paxton himself who were inventors of all that happened here. No longer were Frenchmen imported to put their own stamp on the designs, as in the 1690s; no more restless Lancelot Browns arrived to plan changes in the landscape, in the style he used in countless other places. Chatsworth now had its own inimitable team. Over the next thirty-two years the Duke and Paxton combined enthusiasm and horticultural skill with an abiding love of the place to develop and embellish their own garden, making it like no other in the kingdom. The Duke always described Paxton's achievements generously, giving him credit for the astonishing creations they planned together.

The West Garden

Paxton and Wyatville must have worked together over the West Garden and other projects on the go in the late 1820s, and we know that Paxton was instrumental, with the Duke, in changing Wyatville's plans for what is now the Orangery. Paxton combined tact with persuasiveness, and without appearing to trespass on Wyatville's territory he surely influenced Wyatville in the work in the West Garden wherever architecture impinged on plants. Such an observant man must have learned a lot from watching the North Wing take shape and he soon became a builder himself.

In 1826 the reconstruction of the West Garden was begun and its architectural bones remain unaltered today. We are lucky that our rooms look over it to the river, park and distant woods. Our view is beyond criticism. The ground was levelled again (Brown and Co. had 'sloped' it to the water's edge). Wyatville enclosed it on three sides by a new wall linking Cibber's sphinxes once more and joining the long retaining wall under the West Front of the house and he resuscitated the seventeenth-century pond. This gave an area of just under four and a half acres ready to be planted. The Bachelor Duke wrote: 'This space, flanked by the two large bastions, from its size was difficult to fill and adorn, but Sir Jeffry Wyatville's most ingenious

Above Looking over the West Garden and park from a bedroom on the first floor.

Below One of the yew hedges, planted by Andrew in the 1960s as windbreaks, that divides the West Garden into three sections.

architectural parterres have gone a great way towards it, and the Tulip fountain has lately given life and animation to the centre. The whole forms a support and a platform, that connect and harmonise the buildings of Chatsworth to the utmost advantage.'

There are eight 'ingenious architectural parterres', referred to elsewhere as *'raised stone flower baskets'*, each 40 feet across and 3 feet high. Quite big as flower baskets go. In the corners are golden yews, yellow cushions which fold themselves over the stone and are beacons of light on dark days. One received a direct hit from a firework at the celebration for the Tercentenary of the Dukedom in 1994. It was burnt and is only now beginning to shoot again from its base. Until a few years ago the stone baskets were filled with bedded-out plants. They were not satisfactory, so we planted sharply clipped box and a central green yew, which show up the golden cushions and seem to answer better.

The long narrow enclosure that is the West Garden made a tunnel for the disagreeable north wind, so my husband Andrew suggested planting yew hedges to divide it into three in the 1960s. In the central division is the round pond and the Tulip Fountain fed from the Cascade. The same water gives three displays. It tumbles down the Cascade to vanish at its foot, thence it is piped underground to play the Sea Horse Fountain, is piped again to the Tulip Fountain in the west garden and flows underground once more to reach the river.

The West Garden seems to be the place for royal trees. *'Here stand two imperial trees,'* wrote the Duke; *'planted by the brothers Nicholas* [later Czar Nicholas I] *and Michel Paulowitsch; the first, a Spanish chestnut, promises to be of surpassing beauty.'* It has not fulfilled that promise, but it is indeed of surpassing interest, being a living link with a visit of the future Emperor in 1816, when the two young men became such great friends. The Grand Duke Michael's tree is the variegated sycamore which stands south of the pond opposite Nicholas's chestnut.

The tradition continues. Her Majesty The Queen planted an English oak in 1968 and The Princess of Wales echoed the choice of the Czar by planting another Spanish chestnut when she came here for a Barnardo's garden party attended by 8,000 people in 1986.

Not far away, above what is now the turbine house, are three trees commemorating another Royal visit. The Duke wrote on 20 October 1832, *'Dss Kent and Princess Victoria to Chatsworth. ... Trees ready to be planted below* [the South Terrace]. *Both charmed to plant — Mother a chestnut and Va an oak. The water works were illuminated and nothing was ever so beautiful and between acts they were charged with different coloured Bengal lights and it was quite different from anything I ever saw and*

Above and left The 1820s stone 'flower baskets' in the West Garden, now filled with green box and yew. The clipped and bound Irish yews define the path.

Below and opposite top The architectural plan of the basement of Chiswick House, in London, built by the 3rd Earl of Burlington in 1725, was the source for the design in box in the West Garden. Burlington was inspired by Palladio.

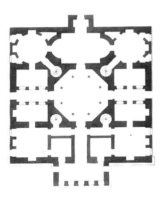

Opposite below Seventeenth-century stairs with remarkable stone frostwork lead down to the West Garden. In front of the Tulip Pond is a nineteenth-century Italian marble lion with Cupid on its back. Lady's mantle (*Alchemilla mollis*) and verbascum are allowed to seed themselves in the cracks between the paving.

beat Petershoff.' Princess Victoria's Journal for the same day records: *'When we had come on the terrace the Duke wished us to plant two trees down under the terrace. So we did, I planted an oak and Mamma a Spanish chesnut.'*[27] The thirteen-year-old Princess dined with the grown-ups for the first time on this visit. Her host ordered a cooked rehearsal the night before. Princess Victoria's Journal 24 October 1832 noted: *'1/4 past 9. We have just left Chatsworth, but not without great regret; we had been so happy there ...'*[28] Mother's chestnut and Va's oak continue to thrive – the latter measured 11 feet in circumference at 5 feet high in 1999. We save acorns from it every year and keep a stock of 'Queen's oaks' to plant in the park and elsewhere. Eleven years later Prince Albert planted a sycamore next to them, so the whole family is aboreally represented within a few feet of each other.

The seventeenth-century stairs and walls of superb frostwork below the house remained untouched till the winters of 1997 and 1999, when they were restored. Nadauld's two stone heads in niches are so like my father they give me quite a turn. Mimulus appears in the cracks in the paving stones; so do sisyrinchium, gentians and the ubiquitous lady's mantle (*Alchemilla mollis*). The plants in the border along the park wall to the west have to be on the scale of their surroundings – artichokes, onopordon, tall shrub roses, hollyhocks, thalilctrum, phloxes, verbascum, echinops, *Clematis* 'Lasurstern', and several varieties of that old stand-by lavatera, of which the 'Barnsley' variety is the best by far. *Crambe cordifolia*, hardy geraniums, delphiniums galore and *Acanthus spinosus* complete the crowded patch, with pelargoniums along the front and pinks and thyme spilling over the stone edge.

We inherited a dreary mess of evergreen shrubs around the pond, but could not decide how to replace them till it occurred to me, while leaning over a show case containing the architectural plan of the basement of Lord Burlington's Chiswick House, that we could use his design to transform the lawn below our windows. In 1960 the scheme was carried out in golden box. The nurserymen had difficulty in finding 3,300 of them to fulfil the order, saying no one had wanted it for sixty years. The design has puzzled people ever since because it is difficult to see the reason for the lines, rounds and squares till the origin of the design is explained. It falls into place once you see the original ground plan and realise that the pond represents the dome and the 'rooms' are divided by 'walls' of box with passages and openings for doors. It makes a dazzling effect, when seen from the west windows above, before it is shorn of its new bright gold leaves in June.

The television programme *The Antiques Roadshow* was filmed here in 1996 and the various experts set up their stalls in the West Garden. People used the 'rooms' as they would have done had they really been in Chiswick House, queueing along the passages and through the doorways. Hundreds came and so careful were they that not a single plant was damaged.

Two lead statues, English seventeenth-century copies after the Antique, stand on the stone edge of the raised border under the park wall. The Borghese Gladiator is defending himself with a shield and a dagger from Hercules, who is for ever trying to bash him with his club. A few years ago these belligerents were hoisted over the wall by a crane to a waiting lorry and driven to a lead hospital for repair – just like the humans they represent, but alas their treatment was not free.

The garden at Chatsworth is not all digging, planting and weeding: it is also a continual round of rescue and repair of what are now heaped together as 'built features'. Authority plays a part here. We are not allowed to move a statue in the garden without planning permission and nearly got into trouble in 1993 when Cibber's Flora returned to her Temple after 180 years in the open without the necessary passport of approval. In the days before we

Above The Borghese Gladiator, an English seventeenth-century figure after the Antique, in the West Garden border, eternally defending himself from Hercules, *opposite*. The gladiator's heel has been mercilessly chewed by a badger.

had to reckon with planning permission the two stone lions' heads were brought from a cottage in Buxton and the stone seat by the wall, moved from the Conservatory Garden, was the answer to a request from Paddy Leigh Fermor for an outdoor place to write. His stony desk is from a farmhouse dairy. I don't believe he has ever used seat or table, but you never know when they might come in handy. There is the usual complement of stone animals near the pond. The bitch and her puppy is a nineteenth-century copy of an original in the Museo Pio Clementino at the Vatican. I didn't know Popes went in for breeding dogs.

Andrew has planted thousands of crocuses and colchicums round the stone baskets and under the Russians' trees. He has spent many hours armed with a trowel and his plan of what was to be planted where and the result is pure pleasure. *Crocus laevigatus* is the first to appear soon after Christmas, followed by all the *Crocus chrysanthus*, which flower from January to May, along with *Crocus imperati, tommasinianus, sieberi* and also *minimus*, which spreads quickly. Some of the flowers are so insignificant they have to be searched for on hands and knees. The autumn-flowering colchicum bulbs arrive in August and must be planted straight away. It is hard work in a dry summer to get these big bulbs into the rock-hard ground, but well worth the effort for the October display. Andrew has often told me that he would like to be remembered by these spring and autumn shows.

The trouble with crocus is their fatal attraction to pheasants, squirrels and mice. The yellow ones are irresistible to all three. An epicurean cock pheasant can destroy an extraordinary number of crocus flowers in a few hours. He is followed up by an odious grey squirrel which finishes the job by digging up the bulbs, leaving a neat hole and much disappointment. The mauve ones survive better, but even they are not safe.

The pace of change at Chatsworth during the twenty years from 1830 reflects Paxton's phenomenal energy and the Duke's ready agreement and growing enthusiasm for all his suggestions. Together they planned the construction of hot houses and the purchase of vast numbers of plants, including forest trees, fruit trees, hardy plants and bulbs then available in this country. They bought rarities from abroad and joined in the thrilling gamble of sending their own employees to the ends of the earth to bring back the exotics that they loved.

The Duke had put Paxton in charge of forestry in 1829, and straightaway the Pinetum was added by enclosing eight acres from the park at the south end of the garden, and in 1835 the Arboretum was commenced. Forty acres were planted with 1,670 species arranged by families.

Among the trees and shrubs planted in 1829–30 was an outstanding curiosity. A weeping ash, already forty years old, was dug up from a nursery garden in Derby and brought the

Above Hercules swinging his club, in the direction of the Borghese Gladiator, opposite. The plants in the border behind the two lead figures include Rosa 'Albertine', *Delphinium* Black Knight Group and *D.* 'Blue Jay', *Geranium psilostemon* and *G.* 'Ann Folkard', *Sisyrinchium striatum, Thalictrum flavum* subsp. *glaucum, Crambe cordifolia,* Russell hybrid lupins and 'Mrs Sinkins' pinks.

Opposite Wisteria macrobotrys cascading over the ferns on the stone seat on the West Drive.

Top Paddy's table in the West Garden, surrounded by geranium, sisyrinchium, thalictrum and thyme.

Above Rosa 'Climbing Abel Chatenay' on the iron balustrade overlooking the West Garden.

Top A nineteenth-century Italian marble goat and kid, after the Antique in the West Garden.

Above Colchicum 'Waterlily', planted by Andrew at the foot of one of the 'stone baskets' in the West Garden.

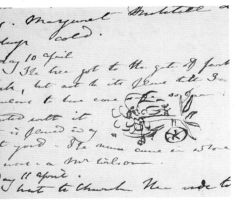

twenty-eight miles to Chatsworth on a 'machine' invented for the purpose by Paxton. Eight tons of earth in a huge ball surrounded the 28-feet-long roots and the journey took three days. It travelled roots first and people hurried out of their houses to see the strange phenomenon rumble by. Twenty men were detailed to accompany it and they managed to manoeuvre it through the narrow toll gates without incident, but gates and walls at the entrance of the park had to be taken down to allow it to pass. On 9 April 1830 the Duke wrote, '*Good Friday. Up at 6 in hope tree would come but it did not all day*'. The following day, '*The tree got to the gate of the park at 11 o.c. but not to its place till 9. It is miraculous to have come safe so far. I was enchanted with it and its place in my courtyard.*' It still grows on its mound by the North Front door 169 years later; it is hollow now and I fear for its survival with every westerly gale. Whoever has the job of cutting it up when it eventually blows over will find a harvest of honey in the trunk, as it has been nature's bee hive for the fifty years I have known it. The weeping ash is the last to put on leaves in spring – '*just a bunch of sticks till June*' is how this historic tree was dismissed by our nanny, whose nursery overlooked it. In 1999 it is 50 feet high and its girth is 8 feet 10½ inches at 5 feet high.

This is another crocus-filled place where one or other of a number of species is in flower from December till the fritillaries follow in May. Andrew plants so many and always in the same place that his spade slices the old to make room for the new. Close by is the tulip tree (*Liriodendron tulipifera*) avenue which runs from the Lodge to the North Front door. It must have been planted when the Wyatville wing was built about 1827. I wonder if these Americans are the most northerly in England?

Since 1828, two years after his arrival, Paxton had begun to experiment with the construction of greenhouses for tender plants and by 1832 twenty-two hot houses and forcing pits had been built in the kitchen garden at Barbrook. Four were for pineapples, several for peaches and cucumbers. There were vineries and a mushroom house. (One peach house contained the finest 'Royal George' peach tree in the country with a 70-feet spread which produced 850 fruit in 1842.) An idea of just how much labour was entailed is given by the fact that one young gardener's sole duty for a whole week in December 1848 was sponging the leaves of a cinnamon tree. This gardener was Robert Aughtie, a rare bird in that he kept a diary from 1848 to 1850 which gives a day-to-day account of the life of an under-gardener in a big establishment 150 years ago. He even records his mistakes. On 21 November 1849: '*Wednesday – Smoked the cucumber house – gave it too much, which caused the plants to loose many of their leaves.*'[29]

Paxton experimented with glass, iron and wood, using great quantities of coal to warm the air in imitation of the tropics, at little cost as the Duke owned nearby mines. The results of his twin passions for engineering and plants were soon to be envied and copied (not always successfully) all over the country.[30]

After a visit to a horticultural show in London in the early 1830s, the Duke came away inspired by the sight of the butterfly orchid, *Psychopsis papilio* (known then as *Oncidium papilio*), from South America. He immediately started to buy orchids, which necessitated three more hot houses being built especially for them, one of which still stands and is now the Vinery. Orchids remained a passion of the Duke and his gardener, and he soon had the most extensive collection in any private garden in the kingdom.

To record his first love of the family Orchidaceae the distinctive flower of the butterfly orchid is carved into the gilded frames which Wyatville designed for the pictures in the Gold Drawing Room (now our dining room) at Chatsworth. The trellis pattern with a single flower protruding from each little triangle and quandrangle succeeds in deceiving the eye into imagining that all the frames are the same size – which they are not. The object of this and the rest of the ornate decoration was to divert attention from the fact that nothing in the room is symmetrical. It succeeds perfectly. There is so much to look at that the irregularities pass unnoticed except by the keenest observer, and the much-loved butterfly orchid flowers are a vital part of the scheme.

Encouraged by the success of his hot houses, Paxton looked to the Orient for further acquisitions. The ingenious invention of Dr Nathaniel Ward, a GP practising in the East End of London, came at the right time for the new discoveries. The Wardian case was a glazed airtight box on a wooden base with glass sides strengthened by wooden struts and a glass top. The safe transport and live delivery of plants from the tropics and elsewhere was now ensured. Till then the mortality rate, because of wildly fluctuating temperatures and dousing by sea water on board ship, had been disheartening to say the least and only a tiny percentage of plants survived the long journeys. Dr Ward's cases changed all that and the loss of the tenderest plant from the steaming jungle or some mountain rarity became the exception rather than the rule. This major step forward encouraged ever more plant-hunting expeditions in search of new specimens and Paxton was, as usual, to the fore. He soon had a reason to send his own man to the East.

A plant the Duke longed to possess, as yet unknown in Europe, was the scarlet-flowered leguminous sacred tree of the Burma teak forest, the *Amherstia nobilis*. After an exchange of letters with Dr Wallich, the director of the Calcutta Botanical Garden (and the discoverer of the amherstia in a monastery garden by the Salween River on the Burma/Siam border), it was arranged that Paxton should send one of his Chatsworth apprentices, 'the intelligent gardener' John Gibson, to India to bring back this prize and other plants. Gibson had a specialist's interest in orchids, and were he successful in trekking as far as their native habitat he might find some of the many that were known to abound.

In 1835 the Duke arranged for him to travel on the ship taking Lord Auckland, who was going out to India as Governor General. Young Gibson (he was only twenty) took with him a consignment of medicinal plants badly needed by Dr Wallich. They were packed in Wardian cases and the gardener and his charges arrived safely at Calcutta. The amherstia was in flower in the Botanical Garden and Gibson was said to have *'run round it clapping his hands like a boy who has got three runs at a cricket match'*. Dr Wallich reported to the Duke, *'As soon as possible after the rainy season has commenced next month, Gibson will proceed to the Khosea range of hills to a place called Chirra Poonje, where he is to remain at least two months making excursions in all directions; collecting and forwarding successfully his harvest (Your Grace's property) of which good care shall be taken in this garden, and on his return bringing whole boatloads with him. I have been on that range lately in October and November last, on my way across that part of the country to Assam, and I can declare with truth that the imagination cannot depict to itself a richer country in botanical varieties; above all, in Orchideous plants.'*

There was neither road nor track to the far-away garden of Eden, so Gibson had to wait for the annual rains to fill the tributaries of the Brahmapootrah River to enable him to get there. In a letter to Mrs Wright (maid to Miss Emily Eden,[31] sister of Lord Auckland), he writes of butterflies innumerable, fifty new parasite plants already secured and, *'in short I tell you Mrs Wright that I am in my glory you will excuse me entering into further details'*.

Gibson returned to Calcutta the following year and was home in 1837. He had collected over a hundred new types of orchids including *Dendrobium densiflorum, Vanda* (now *Trudelia*) *alpina, Cymbidium devonianum, Pleione praecox* and other hitherto unknown plants from the *'fabulous Ind'*.

Above One of the orchids, a *Paphiopedilum* hybrid, growing at Chatsworth today.

Below The 6th Duke's favourite orchid, known to him as *Oncidium papilio*, appears hundreds of times in the trellis of the gilded picture frames designed by Wyatville in our dining room.

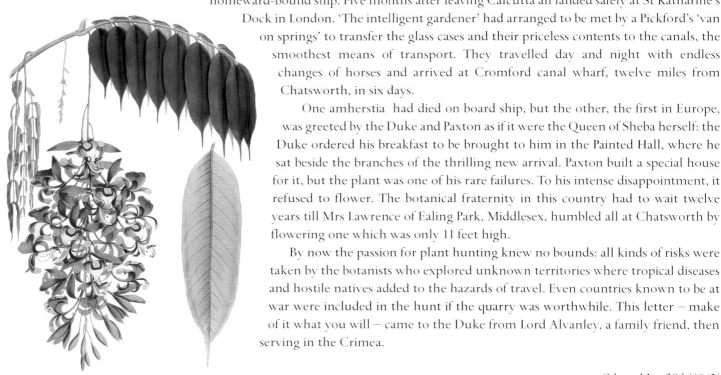

The amherstia was not among them (he would have had to journey on to Burma to retrieve it from the wild) but Dr Wallich gave Gibson two plants from the Botanical Garden, which were carefully packed and placed with twelve cases of orchids on the poop deck of the homeward-bound ship. Five months after leaving Calcutta all landed safely at St Katharine's Dock in London. 'The intelligent gardener' had arranged to be met by a Pickford's 'van on springs' to transfer the glass cases and their priceless contents to the canals, the smoothest means of transport. They travelled day and night with endless changes of horses and arrived at Cromford canal wharf, twelve miles from Chatsworth, in six days.

One amherstia had died on board ship, but the other, the first in Europe, was greeted by the Duke and Paxton as if it were the Queen of Sheba herself: the Duke ordered his breakfast to be brought to him in the Painted Hall, where he sat beside the branches of the thrilling new arrival. Paxton built a special house for it, but the plant was one of his rare failures. To his intense disappointment, it refused to flower. The botanical fraternity in this country had to wait twelve years till Mrs Lawrence of Ealing Park, Middlesex, humbled all at Chatsworth by flowering one which was only 11 feet high.

By now the passion for plant hunting knew no bounds: all kinds of risks were taken by the botanists who explored unknown territories where tropical diseases and hostile natives added to the hazards of travel. Even countries known to be at war were included in the hunt if the quarry was worthwhile. This letter – make of it what you will – came to the Duke from Lord Alvanley, a family friend, then serving in the Crimea.

Above Amherstia nobilis *as illustrated in Paxton's* Magazine of Botany.

Odessa May 29th [1842]

Dear Duke

My sister wrote from Nice to desire me to get certain plants for you ... which you believed I might find in the Crimea. The following is the result of my inquiries at the Imperial botanical Garden in that country, from which I have just returned. The Gentiana caucasia might be had if a botanist was sent to the coast to collect it, as it is near the Russian lines; but the Gentiana fimbriata, humilis, umbellata and the Primula amoena are only to be had by sending a contingent of 10000 infantry, six light mountain guns, & some hundred irregular horse to fetch them. I have no doubt that the emperor would allow such an expedition to rendezvous at Anapa, if he was informed of the importance of the object in view, but as my commission did not go so far as to authorise me to commence negotiations on the subject, I shall wait further instructions from you before I do so en attendant. I send you some plants from the garden at Nikita which, I believe, you will be glad to have. A young man who served under your gardener at Chatsworth assisted Mr Hartwiss the director of the establiment in his choice, & I now enclose you a list of them. In addition to what are marked in it you will find in the smaller box some bulbs of the Galanthus plicatus ... I am informed that they ought to have been planted & allowed to blow, previously to their being sent, I shall have some others properly treated, & sent in the month of July. I also enclose you a list of plants which the Director of the Garden at Nikita wishes to have, & which I have no doubt you will be glad to send him if you have them. I hope my envoi will arrive safe & alive, & that this will make up for the temporary disappointment about the Gentiana, as I do not doubt, that you will not scruple a moment to take the steps I have above alluded to to get them. Adieu Dear Duke, write me a line here to say that you have received this and another to thank Mr Hartwiss for his civility ... .

Yours Always,

Alvanley.

By 1836 the Bachelor Duke was very proud of his collection. On 2 August he was '*Drunk with Chatsworth. The new walls, the House so improved and perfect.*' Four days later: '*Drove in britchka on two tired post horses to Kitchen Garden ... Nobody ever can come up to me about plants.*'

On 29 August he was '*Up early. At Kitchen Garden — treasures there! Busy with Sir W Hooker's Hibiscus.*' But he also had some unlucky experiences. On 1 October 1835: '*Poor Paxton great disapt. today. Henderson, Mr Lowe and my collector having returned with but few plants being too ill and beset with the fevers of the country to remain in Mexico. A great vexation.*' Collecting mania made him very upset when someone else got the prize. On 29 October 1835: '*Paxton and I very low about Forbes getting all Prince John* [Joseph] *Dyck's cactus.*' On the other hand he was the recipient of generous presents from friends and neighbours, including some rarities from Sir Oswald Mosley of Rolleston Hall.

Above Coelogyne wallichiana (now *Pleione praecox*) as illustrated in Paxton's *Magazine of Botany.*

Below A Wardian case, the invention which enabled delicate plants to travel thousands of miles and arrive alive.

Another subject for collection and introduction to these islands was the rich variety of trees from the north-west coast of the Americas. Following Gibson's successful excursion to India, the Duke and Paxton got up a syndicate of interested people to send a similar expedition to this virgin country where travellers had seen, but had retrieved little, of all sorts of arboreal wonders growing there. Again Chatsworth garden provided the men to lead the collectors of seeds and cones, and Robert Wallace (whose wife went with him) and Peter Banks left England in 1838. After crossing Canada and the Rockies disaster struck — their canoe hit a rock in turbulent waters on the Columbia River. All on board were drowned. Paxton wrote to the Duke on 29 May 1839: '*Last Thursday I received the melancholy news of the untimely deaths of Robt Wallace and Peter Banks ... Poor old Wallace and his wife bear the loss much better than I could have expected.*' The Duke, in Geneva, was deeply shocked, replying with typical generosity and concern for the bereaved, on 8 June 1839: '*Wallace had only one anxiety when he took leave of me, it was about his parents if anything shd happen to him — and I promised him that they should want nothing. That is a sacred promise and I rely on you to see it executed. I should like to get them a house near Chatsworth — it is too far for the old man to go every day.*' After this tragedy neither Paxton nor his principal had the heart to be associated with any more plant-hunting expeditions.

The giant redwood, or Wellingtonia (*Sequoiadendron giganteum*), and its less attractive relation, the coastal redwood (*Sequoia sempervirens*), were two of the trees that Wallace and Banks might have found had they reached their goal. They were eventually brought back by William Lobb, who was collecting for Messrs Veitch, in 1853. *Sequoiadendron giganteum* and the boring old Lawson cypress (*Chamaecyparis lawsoniana*), introduced in 1854, are planted on the banks surrounding the site of the old conservatory. They are a constant reminder to me of poor Wallace and Banks and of the risks taken by the plant hunters of the nineteenth century, so many of whom perished far from home.

The story of the *Victoria amazonica* from South America has a happier ending. This extraordinary water lily was seen by a traveller in Peru in 1801 and was recorded again on the Amazon in 1832, but it was the traveller and plant hunter Sir Robert Schomburgk who sent the first full description in 1837, this time from British Guyana. In 1846 seeds arrived at Kew, but, although its immense, saucer-like, leathery leaves with their upturned rims grew vigorously, it behaved as the amherstia had at Chatsworth and would not flower.

Paxton begged a plant from Sir William Hooker, director of the Botanic Gardens at Kew, and built a special tank for it in the kitchen garden near his own house. The little seedling he brought from London in 1849 in a box $13^{1}/_{2} \times 8$ inches gave scant warning of the giant it was soon to become — six weeks later the lily's leaves were 3 feet 6 inches in diameter and 11

Above left Seen early in the season, before its leaves have grown to their full size, is the *Victoria amazonica* in the Display Greenhouse.

Above right 'Victoria Regia', as illustrated by Walter Fitch in 1851. Like so much at Chatsworth, the lily has had more than one name.

feet in circumference. On 1 October they had grown to 4 feet and by 15 October had added 5 more inches. The tank had to be enlarged to accommodate its giant tenant. Lo and behold, on 2 November an enormous bud appeared and Paxton was beside himself with delight. The *'sight is worth a journey of a thousand miles,'* he wrote to Sir William Hooker.

The Duke was at Lismore in Ireland. He hurried home to see for himself the latest botanical miracle. Violet Markham, Paxton's grand-daughter, tells the story.[33] ' *"All the world comes to look,"* the Duke remarked. *Among the visitors were the Duke's friends, Lady Hunloke and Lady Newburgh, and Sir William Hooker and Dr Lindley from Kew. The enormous leaves were supported on the outside by the network of radiating ribs described by Sir Robert Schomburgk. This vegetable cellular system gave the leaf strength and unique power of flotation. Its carrying capacities were put to a practical test. On November 22nd Paxton's youngest daughter, Annie, then aged seven, was put on one of the leaves by the Duke and Lady Newburgh. Hooker was incredulous on hearing the story, but Paxton writes to confirm its truth. The leaf was able to sustain a weight of a hundred pounds. The little girl, dressed like a fairy, made a pretty picture.*

'Victoria continued to oblige. By September the following year she had produced 140 leaves and 112 flower buds. Also what Paxton described as "fine plump seeds", from which a large number of strong plants were raised.' The flowering of the giant water lily was the result of Paxton's unerring attention to detail. He added a little water wheel to the tank, which made a gentle movement in imitation of the slow-moving waters of the inlets of the Amazon where the lily grew. His reward was immediate. The lily was called 'Victoria Regia' after the Queen, who, on 13 November 1849, was pleased to receive Paxton bearing a flower and a leaf as a gift to his sovereign. (Later it reverted to its first name *Victoria amazonica*.)

Violet Markham continues, *'But this development, rapid and unexpected as it had been, brought other problems in its train. Twice she had outgrown her tank; a new house fitting for her maturity had to be devised. Paxton … had been experimenting for years with glass-houses. He had built them in all sizes, shapes and designs. But he did not repeat himself on this occasion. He struck out a fresh line to meet the needs of his precious lily. In about three months, at the cost of £800, he produced a novel type of conservatory, 61 feet long by 49 feet broad. This held a circular tank 33 feet in diameter.'* It was built at the north end of the old kitchen garden close to Paxton's house at Barbrook. No sign is left of either building now.

'The house, built entirely of glass and iron with a roof on the ridge-and-furrow principle, had new and

special features. Perfect facilities for drainage and ventilation were required. For this the new house provided that the roof was not only a roof, but a light and heat adjuster; the iron columns were not columns, but drain pipes; rafters and sash bars served the same purpose. The floor was not only a floor, but at the same time a ventilator and a dust trap.

'Multiply these principles in a building, covering not sixty feet but eighteen acres, weld glass and iron together by girders above and below, and what emerges is — the Crystal Palace.'

Violet Markham goes on to quote her grandfather, who read a paper describing his design to the Fine Arts Society on 13 November 1850. *'He exhibited one of the marvellous leaves five feet in diameter and pointed out that its underside was a beautiful example of natural engineering. For it possessed ribs like cantilevers radiating from the centre (where they were nearly two inches deep), with large bottom flanges, and very thin middle ribs with cross girders between each pair to keep the middle ribs from buckling. "Nature was the engineer," said Paxton. "Nature has provided the leaf with longitudinal and transverse girders and supports that I, borrowing from it, have adopted in this building."'* He was describing his Crystal Palace.

Below The Lily House at Barbrook, Chatsworth, at the turn of the century. Sadly it no longer exists.

'O Paxton!'

The later years of the 6th Duke

1835—1858

Previous pages Part of Paxton's massive Rock Garden.

By the mid-1830s everything seemed possible and the plans which Paxton had in mind were bigger and better than those which had gone before. His employer had complete confidence in him and gave him the free rein he needed.

An ever-increasing number of tender plants arrived at Chatsworth and it was decided to build a conservatory which would contain them and allow for their rapid growth. The scale would be like all else at Chatsworth – gigantic.

Above The Great Conservatory showing clearly the ridge-and-furrow construction. The figure between the two evergreens to the left of the entrance gives an idea of the scale of the building.

The Great Conservatory

In 1836 the foundation stone of the Great Conservatory was laid by Lord Burlington, the Duke's heir. Three years later the first planting took place and it was completed in the winter of 1840–41. In this latest, and largest, building by Paxton at Chatsworth he was *'ably assisted'* by Decimus Burton, who went on to be architect of, among other well-known landmarks, the Palm House at Kew.

The conception was vast. Trees were felled and an area 400 x 213 feet was levelled to make a site on which the building stood. *'You perceive that the situation is perfectly well adapted, being sheltered on all sides by high trees: it was, indeed, cleared out of the heart of the wood; yet, strange to say, far as it was from any habitation, traces were discovered underground of walls, and flues much used, and some fragments of fluted columns.'* No explanation of these intriguing finds described by the Duke has ever been made. The biggest glasshouse in England had room inside for two carriages to pass on the main thoroughfare, and stairs, hidden by ascending rocks, led to a gallery from which you could inspect the highest branches of the exotic palms and other trees flourishing there. There were ponds full of aquatic plants, rocks, mosses, ferns and brilliantly coloured flowers in a tropical climate which was so ventilated that it was not uncomfortable.

The building itself was 277 feet long, 123 feet wide, 61 feet high and covered just over three-quarters of an acre. There were eight underground boilers fuelled by coal which arrived by underground trams. You can see a short length of tram line in a cave by the Strid Pond and grills, still there in the lawn on the west side of the building, allowed air to the boilers below which fed a seven-mile maze of 6-inch hot-water pipes. There were forty miles of sash bars which joined panes of glass 4 feet long by 6 inches wide placed diagonally to that of the horizontal plane in the style of ridge and furrow, made and supplied by Robert Chance of Birmingham. It cost £33,099. It was described at the time as a *'mountain of glass', 'an unexampled structure' 'like a sea of glass when the waves are settling and smoothing down after a storm, which is the result of its undulating structure'.*[34] The King of Saxony compared it to a *'tropical scene with a glass sky'.*[35]

Even the Duke found it difficult to describe. *'It is not a thing to be described, and all my attempt will be to enable you to see, and make others see, what it contains with the least fatigue and trouble. Its success has been complete, both for the growth of plants and the enjoyment it affords, being, I believe, the only hothouse known, to remain in which longer than ten minutes does not produce a state of suffering. In consequence also of the subterranean furnaces, to which a railway conducts the coal, there is the remarkable feature of cleanliness, and absence of smoke and smell, unknown in any other building of the kind.'*

Every winter the furnaces consumed 300 tons of coal and coke – considerably more than that used in the house, but then the welfare of the exotics in the conservatory was more important than that of mere humans. The smoke passed through an underground flue which ran up the hill for 265 yards and came out via a conventional chimney 58 feet high in Stand Wood, over the garden wall, thereby keeping the surroundings clean and free of smoke. The beeches in the wood now are higher than the chimney, so it is hidden.

The Handbook gives us a vivid picture of the tropical luxuriance to be found inside. *'I begin my enumeration on the right side of the middle road. There are orange-trees beginning to be acclimated; an Altingia of still more rapid growth than usual, and Araucarias that ere long will have gained the roof, and were only planted to fill the space for a time; the Walton date-palm, growing every day more like that of Posilippo; Hibiscus splendens; Erythrina arborea, Palmettos, Plantains; the Walton Corypha umbraculifera, now only beginning to recover from its journey; the various creepers and passiflorae; Bougainvillia spectabliis; and Stephanotis floribunda, ascending even to the roof. Here is Sagus [Cycas?] Rumphii, most rare, and Bambusia arundinacea growing with an extraordinary luxuriance that justifies its presence here, over-shadowing both sides of the road. Returning by it, you must now observe Sabal Blackburniana, the very first stove-plant I acquired, from the collection of Mrs Beaumont of the North; then Cocos plumosa, easily surpassing all others, a present from the Sheffield Horticultural Society; the Rose Hibiscus, and more lofty Musae. Beyond the division you see a sort of jungle, in which some Cassias and Hibiscus mutabilis predominate; the Banyan tree, and the obstinate Ficus elastica, so vigorous and overbearing in its former house, so languid here; Lord Fitzwilliam's present, Dracaena Draco, that promises to rival the Dragon tree of Java. Other Phoenixes, and the gigantic Fourcroyas, are among the innumerable occupiers of the rocks contrived to hide the gallery staircase: what chiefly promises to cover and clothe them is Ficus repens, of rapid, searching growth.'*

We may not share his love of *Ficus elastica* and *Ficus repens* (now known as *Ficus pumila*), having seen them too often in the hideous surroundings of the halls of modern office blocks, but one must remember the excitement of the new a hundred and fifty years ago.

At the north-west corner a hedge of aloes reminded people of the shores of the Mediterranean. It served as a fence to halt the *'inquisitive public'* as it was impossible to admit all the *'48,000 visitors here'.*

Above An ivy-covered urn beside one of the two archways that lead into the Great Conservatory Garden. Little else is left of Paxton's masterpiece at Chatsworth.

A hand-coloured photograph taken in 1890 of the carriage drive through the Great Conservatory.

Once again the enormous effort of transporting exotics is described and dismissed as being *'rather expensive'*. *'A conspicuous Palmetto (Chamaerops humilis), and the finest Zamia in the world, both of these from the Tankerville collection'*. The zamia weighed twelve tons and was brought from Surrey. *'It was a great work to remove the treasures of that place: in order to do it, their house had to be pulled down, and then it had to be built up again. Carriages were invented and contrived, and turnpike gates demolished for their passage; so that this present was rather an expensive one: Baron Ludwig's was less costly. The variety of Zamias in it deserve the appellation of venerable, and, with the monster Testudinarias at the kitchen-garden, formed a valuable cargo, that was nearly shipwrecked, and completely drenched with sea-water for a long period, on board the Reliance, a ship totally wrecked in the following year, on her return on the same voyage from the Cape. The plants' adventures did not end here, for such was the irregularity of the traffic then on the newly-opened railway, that they were sent in three directions, and during the coldest frost, to Sheffield, Nottingham and Leeds. They have all recovered, though some for years betrayed no sign of life.'*

The hazardous journeys and the danger of losing everything including the crew in shipwrecks made importations from abroad a risky business, whether it was plants or the Duke's adored sculptures by Canova and others from Italy. The Duke's descriptions of waiting on tenterhooks for the safe arrival of the cargo, whether plants or marbles, remind us of the dangers of travel by sea at that time. *'Proceeding, you find a remarkable group of flowering shrubs, Francisca Hopeana, in great luxuriance, with every variety of Chinese Rose Hibiscus, and Poinsettia pulcherrima most splendid; and a grove of Musa Cavendishii follows, groaning with the weight of fruit, that dwarf Banana, that seldom exceeds six feet in height, and flowers in its second year. The two fine plants of Cycas revoluta have been raised from seed here in my recollection. Next, you find, in the South-east corner, sugar-canes, ripe and prosperous in free soil; Brownia grandiceps, Carica Papaya, and other tropical prodigies. Nearly the most attractive spot of all is that ill nick-named the dismal swamp, a pool surrounded by Papyrus, Arums, Chinese Rush, and Hedychium coronarium. On the rock-work, to which you now return, thrive numerous Cactae; but in still greater richness, on the shady northern side, grows the graceful family of tropical ferns.*

'You ascend the moss-grown, shady steps leading to the gallery, from which alone you can form an idea of the space occupied, and of the health enjoyed by this luxuriant vegetation. It is worth your while to go round the four sides: you will remark contrivances always ready for watering the plants; and here, having admired them from below, you are admitted into the recesses and mysteries of their growth and development.'

Having come down we are reminded by our guide not to leave the house without inspecting other imported curiosities which found a place among the plants, including *'the giant crystal, a mountain of light'* now in the Sculpture Gallery.

Visiting botanists and scientists alike were thrilled with what they found. One of these, Charles Darwin, came to see it in 1845 and wrote on 28 October 1845, *'Finally I visited Chatsworth, with which I was, like a child, transported with delight. Have you ever seen it? Really the great Hot house, & especially the water part, is more wonderfully like tropical nature, than I could have conceived possible. — Art beats nature altogether there.'*[36]

Queen Victoria and Prince Albert came to stay from 1 to 3 December 1843. They invited themselves, at only three weeks' notice. The Duke was quite huffy at the idea, the disruption it would cause and the short time for preparation. On Friday 10 November 1843 he wrote: *'Was getting into carriage to go to Bath ... and the post brought me the news that the Queen wants to come to Chatsworth the end of this month. Ah! a deal of trouble — but it's better over, and now in a dull time than taking a pleasant bit out of my year.'* However, he soon threw himself into the planning with enthusiasm and spared no effort to entertain the Royal couple and make their visit a memorable one. He filled the house to overflowing with family and friends, as well as the inevitable retinue for the Royal guests. Paxton, of course, was master of ceremonies.

The most exciting and surely the most original entertainment — as there was nowhere a building to rival it — was an evening carriage drive in the December darkness to see the new conservatory. The Queen, the Prince and their host entered the brilliantly illuminated garden, decorated with blue, red and green lights, passed below the Cascade, where 'Russian lights' shone in the trees, via the Rock Garden still under construction, to enter the tropical paradise. The plants were already well established and had grown with great speed in the manner of tropical vegetation, some of the trees having reached 40 feet high in only three years. The glass palace was lit by 14,000 lamps hung along the gallery and from the iron ribs of the ridge-and-furrow roof. Her Majesty got out of her carriage and Paxton introduced her and the Prince to the extraordinary variety of hothouse flora. The Queen was delighted and wrote in her Journal: *'the most stupendous and extraordinary creation imaginable ... The whole is entirely of glass. The finest & rarest plants & flowers are in it ... This Conservatory was planned by the Duke's gardener, Mr Paxton, a very clever man ... Mr Paxton is quite a genius, for he plans out all the buildings, as well as laying out his gardens and the Horticultural garden.'*[40]

After the Royal party left, a crowd of 5,000 people who had been given tickets, *'composed of every class of society, from the highest to the humblest, were all admitted without distinction. The rush to the gate was tremendous and the confusion great. The light fingered gentry succeeding in easing the pockets of several persons',*[41] and one of the guests was relieved of his gold watch. Some 30,000 people saw the illuminations and the fireworks from the park, greeting each display with shouts of delight. *'Cannons were fired from the Hunting Tower and a blaze of coloured lights burst from the Robber's Stone* [high above the aqueduct], *waterfall, cascade and fountains till all was enveloped in one sheet of livid light.'* Paxton had outdone himself.

To her uncle, the King of the Belgians, the Queen wrote on 4 December 1843, *'We arrived at Chatsworth on Friday, and left it at nine this morning, quite charmed and delighted with everything there. Splendour and comfort are so admirably combined, and the Duke does everything so well. I found many improvements since I was there eleven years ago. The conservatory is out and out the finest thing imaginable of its kind. It is one mass of glass, 64 feet high, 300' long and 134' wide. The grounds, with all the woods and cascades and fountains, are so beautiful too. The first evening there was a ball, and the next the cascades and fountains were illuminated which had a beautiful effect.'*[38]

George Anson, Private Secretary to Prince Albert, underlined the Queen's enthusiasm in a memorandum of 4 December 1843. *'Today the Queen leaves this magnificent place after a soujourn* [sic] *of 3 nights. The Prince is much struck with it, & pronounces it the finest place he has yet seen belonging to any subject of the Queen. The Duke of Devonshire has been much pleased with the visit & has entered into everything with the greatest spirit & spared no expense or trouble to ensure the visit going off well, & he has succeeded admirably.'*[39]

One of the guests was the Duke of Wellington. He went for an early-morning stroll after the festivities of the night before and was amazed to find no trace of the thousands of visitors and all that had happened. With his usual thoroughness, Paxton himself had led a team of two hundred men who worked all night to clear up the debris as well

Below The interior of the Great Conservatory at the time of Queen Victoria's visit. The doorway in the the rocks (seen on the right) led to the steps up to the viewing gallery which ran all round the building. Bananas, date palms and other tropical trees soon reached the roof so visitors could be close to the top branches of these exciting and rare species. The dwarf banana, *Musa acuminata* 'Cavendishii' is pictured at bottom left.

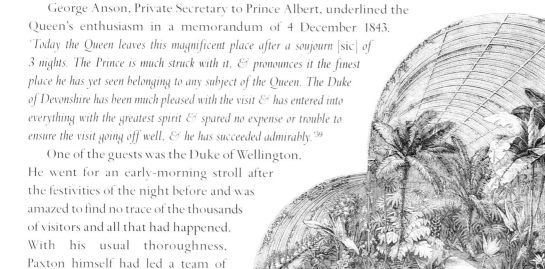

as the fallen December leaves. The place was pristine. Wellington was deeply impressed and remarked to Devonshire, '*I would have liked that man of yours for one of my generals.*'

Lady Palmerston was unable to be present owing to her daughter's confinement, but she heard about the visit and wrote to the Duke, '*How pleased Paxton must be at his success — I hope it won't turn his head — but I believe nothing can.*'

After the 6th Duke died there were no more such extravagant fêtes, but the conservatory was still a big attraction for the thousands of people who came to the garden every year. Nearly half a century passed quietly and the giant greenhouse was put in good order in 1900 by the 8th Duke, who had little interest in plants but was a responsible owner and made sure his properties, however peculiar, were maintained.

It was the Great War of 1914–18 which sealed the fate of the glass building. There was neither men nor coal to service it and it must have been a dismal sight after those years of abandonment when the tropical plants had died of cold and much repair was needed. The profundity of the change of heart after the long and cruel war must be remembered. Ostentation was out and economy was in. Victor, the 9th Duke, decided that such a luxury – it took ten men to look after it – was out of tune with the post-war times and the end of the Conservatory was inevitable. From distant Canada, where he was Governor General from 1916 to 1920, he telegraphed the order to pull it down. So well built was it that it proved impossible, so they decided to use explosives and blow it up (see pages 95–8).

The only glasshouses built by Paxton that remain are the Vinery, near the Potting Shed, and the Conservative Wall, so called because it did and does, conserve heat. It is also known as the Case or the Portland Walk – we go in for several names for the same place, as the Russians do for people, which bemuses newcomers. It was made by the master in 1842 to take the place of the old wooden walk to the stables. It had an ingenious system of flues and hot-water pipes and at first the tender climbers were protected in winter by blue-and-white striped canvas curtains. The glass came later and the middle compartment was added in 1850 by John Robertson, architectural draughtsman to Paxton's old adversary, Loudon (see page 82) and co-architect with Paxton of the surprising cottages in the model village of Edensor, built in 1839–40. The famous pair of *Camellia reticulata* 'Captain Rawes' have grown in this middle section ever since. (The Captain served in the Honourable East India Company and brought the first plant to this country in 1820.) Whether the house was built for them or whether they are planted in the place of honour by chance I do not know. 'Captain Rawes' is difficult to propagate, otherwise I am sure it would be more widely grown. In 1999 the trunk of one of the trees measured 2 feet 3 inches in circumference at 2 feet 6 inches from the ground and that of the other 2 feet 5½ inches at the same height. They have to be trimmed back at the 24-feet-high roof every year. I would dearly love to know what height they would have reached had the roof expanded with their growth. They are beginning to go back a little, but they have delighted their audience here for a hundred and fifty years and have provided decorations difficult to exceed in beauty and originality on many occasions.

They saved the day at our wedding in April 1941. There were no flowers to be bought – people were more interested in survival than selling flowers in that month of savage air raids. So my mother-in-law sent boxes of pink camellias to London on the train to cheer up the drawing room of my parents' house in Rutland Gate, where the reception was held. Three nights before the wedding a bomb fell which destroyed nearby houses in the street and blew out all our windows, so the room would have been bleak indeed without them.

Above Ian Webster, who joined the staff in 1972, cutting 'Alba Plena' camellias in the Conservative Wall. *Overleaf* The Conservative Wall.

Opposite The Conservative Wall houses *Camellia reticulata* 'Captain Rawes', also illustrated (*above*) in *Iconographie du genre Camellia* by Laurenzo Berlèse, Paris 1843.

Below The Wellington Rock, the largest and most impressive of the named 'rocks'. The construction of the Rock Garden was, for Paxton, an uncharacteristically long-drawn-out affair. Digging the nine-acre reservoir and designing and laying the complicated system of pipes for the Emperor Fountain took only six months. So the six years in the making of this part of the garden shows what a vast undertaking it was.

The Rock Garden

I do not know where Paxton got his inspiration for the Rock Garden. Perhaps he brought back memories of the Alps; perhaps he admired the natural rocks of the moorland scenery above the house. Wherever the idea was born work began in 1842 to translate it into reality.

The following year the 6th Duke wrote, '*I must describe it, not as it is now, but as it will be next year: the progress has been rapid. In the Autumn of 1842 there was not a single stone in these parts; you will now find a labyrinth of rocky walks. Dantan jeune[40] was here at the beginning, and, much puzzled, had the kindness to give us a sketch for the better arrangement of the rocks. He would be surprised to see the structure of which the foundations were then laid.*' Once again Paxton invented an 'apparatus' on which the vast stones were moved and winched into place. Later it was borrowed by imitators to move a rock weighing fifty tons. The Duke wrote, '*The spirit of some Druid seems to animate Mr Paxton in these bulky removals.*'

There is a gentle, almost subconscious introduction to the Rock Garden on the path from the Cascade: there are the two piles of stones which are modest in size compared to what is to come. One marks the way to the Copper Tree to the left; the other goes towards the Ring Pond to the right. When the Rock Garden was constructed the Copper Tree of 1695 was copied and made new, by '*an ingenious workman Mr Bower of Chesterfield*' and re-sited in its present position. The Copper Tree – or the Willow Tree – or, best of all, the Squirting Tree (so described by the future Queen Victoria when, aged thirteen, she was delighted by it) is a practical joke of 1695. Every branch spurts out water when it is turned on by the wheel hidden behind the rocks opposite. There used to be pipes in the gravel all around the tree as well as the shower from each branch, so the poor victim of the joke was soaked wherever he stood. In winter, when the real trees have lost their leaves, the sculpted one comes into its own and is indistinguishable from the rest in the grove – all the better for wetting the unsuspecting guest.

Two rocks at the end of the path from the Squirting Tree could pass unnoticed. One is the 'miniature Matterhorn' which is mounted on an invisible metal swivel and turned at the touch of a finger to block the path with its bulk. When Chatsworth was occupied by Penrhos College during the Second World War a schoolgirl was injured by the revolving monster which got such a weigh on it was impossible to stop. Wedges were fixed to prevent further accidents. Its neighbour is so balanced that it rocks up and down with little pressure. I expect lovers of Health and Safety would like this to be prevented from performing as well. Luckily few know about the rocking rock and perhaps it is better so.

Round the next bend you find yourself surrounded by Paxton's gritstone wonderland, a massive monument to the man who could do nothing in a mean way. It is a far cry from the conventional idea of a rock garden where some tufa stones are set up with handfuls of soil to grow miniature plants in imitation of a pocket edition of alpine scenery. It is on a gargantuan scale. You walk under and through the rocks, their great grey tonnage making it hard to believe that they were brought from elsewhere, firstly because of the task of moving such monsters and secondly because they succeed so well in looking as if they have always been there. Some appear to have tumbled from the sky like so many children's bricks and fallen magically into place with no human help, stacked up stone upon stone awaiting a Brobdingnagian toddler to push them over. Some are reminders of creatures from the Lost World, half crocodile, half pterodactyl, sleeping now but about to awake and crush the invader of their territory. Some appear to be crouching, poised ready to lift their vast bulk and fly. In spite of their weight they are so ingeniously placed, with no visible cement, that they look almost delicate in their arrangement. Although constantly threatening, it is not an unfriendly place and people wander happily along the paths pausing on the bridge over the Strid Pond where the trout hope to be fed.

The three named rocks are made up of many big stones. These have indeed been cemented together and you can see the joins. The Duke of Wellington's, at 45 feet high, is much bigger than Queen Victoria's and Prince Albert's, and it has the advantage of its own waterfall from top to bottom, which draws attention to it and is apparently natural. It is not natural at all but a grand kind of stage set. Completing it was cause for celebration among the gardeners. Robert Aughtie wrote in his diary on 13 September 1848, *'Finished the large Wellington rock — had some ale in the evening to christen it — got rather tipsey and was very noisey coming home.'*[41] A pipe hidden in ivy supplies the waterfall. The pond below and the stream which goes under the road to feed the Strid Pond are all part of the scheme to persuade you that you are in a wild and rocky country a thousand miles from civilisation. When there is a frost after heavy rain the waterfall is a magnificent sight, like a thick white beard surrounded by icicles of a yard long, and on a hot day in summer the sound of dripping water is pleasant enough. The pond is flanked by clumps of gunnera, the only plant of a grand enough scale to look right beneath the rock.

Above The copper Willow Tree, described by the thirteen-year-old Princess Victoria as the 'squirting tree'. It is a plumber's responsiblity rather than a gardener's, and never fails to surprise an innocent visitor.

Follow the stream when it reappears from under the road and you will *'Behold the tremendous Strid, where again figures the clearest of streams, a fac-simile of the renowned chasm of the Wharfe, only tamed; and where the saut perilleux may be accomplished without danger or alarm.'* The Strid Pond is a tame copy of the terrifying original near Bolton Abbey, Yorkshire, where the wide River Wharfe suddenly plunges through a narrow channel in the rocks with all its immense force. Called the Strid (or Stride), the gap is little more than a yard wide and almost invites the bold to jump the foaming water, but the slippery rocks sloping the wrong way are extremely dangerous. Under the raging torrent of water are a series of pot holes to a depth of 30 feet and anything, or anybody, falling in rarely surfaces for several days. Many people have been drowned in that legendary place. The pale version in the Rock Garden holds no such danger. Work was still going on here in 1847 when bills were paid for *'setting leaping stones'.* It widens into a tranquil pond where water lilies and bulrushes (*Typhia latifolia*) grow.

'Admire the wild currants from Fountains' Abbey, and do not disdain the collection of our native mosse,' the Duke instructs us. I do not disdain native mosses, a whole world of their own apt to be bundled together. A cryptogam was established by Paxton on the rocks below the Strid. Chatsworth was one of the first gardens in this country to devote an area exclusively to mosses, liverworts and lichens — the primitive flowerless plants which in their vast variety are as fascinating as any full-blown lily or delphinium. Although that area of the rock garden is no longer given over to them there are a number of cool damp spots where they still do well — see the Salisbury lawns for a start. Lichen, particularly, is an indicator of air pollution and has improved in quantity and quality since the demise of the North Derbyshire coal mines and the passing of the Clean Air laws.

I wonder if Granny Evie, my grandmother-in-law, ever read Paxton's rules for rock gardens in his *Magazine of Botany*, set out with his usual authority. He was emphatic in his

Above and left Part of Paxton's magnificent Rock Garden, showing the precarious balancing of huge rocks which was achieved without the benefit of modern machinery or visible cement.

Opposite Plants that grow among the rocks include, *from top left, Gunnera manicata; Primula japonica* 'Postford White'; honeysuckle with *Rosa moyesii;* and *Primula pulverulenta.*

Above The Strid Pond. The planting includes *Typhia latifolia, Gaultheria shallon, Telekia speciosa* and *Heracleum montegazzianum.*
Opposite The Strid.
Below Rhododendrons planted in the 1930s.

aims *'to copy the most picturesque assemblages of natural rocks',* and to ensure that *'the fragments employed are massive'* and, most important, that *'the vegetation which accompanies an extensive rockery be subordinate to it'.*[42] It is the last one which she consciously disagreed with, and I can understand why. Her generation was too close to the Victorians and their fancies.

It seems that the major changes in the garden have taken place every seventy years or so. The 1st Duke's ideas of the 1690s were anathema to his successors in the 1760s, and the Bachelor struck out in an entirely new direction in the 1830s. After the Great Conservatory, the most exaggerated Victorianism of his time was the Rock Garden of the 1840s. Neither was appreciated by Granny Evie when her husband succeeded his uncle in 1908 and it was her turn to run the garden. Seventy years had passed and the art, architecture and gardens of the previous era were best forgotten. To her credit Granny seldom destroyed what she disliked either indoors or out, but masked it as best she could. In the State Rooms she hung cotton curtains over the Bachelor Duke's stamped leather and in the Rock Garden she made haste to plant just the vegetation that Paxton advised against in a successful attempt to blot out the tiresome rocks. Yews and bamboos were her chief aids and quite soon the dramatic shapes were screened and softened so that you could almost pretend the rocks had disappeared. Now we are trying to go back to the inventor's rules. Much vegetation, including trees, have gone lately and the 'picturesque assemblages' are visible once more.

The Emperor Fountain

The Emperor Fountain is the best-known feature of the garden. We owe it to Paxton's genius. It is visible from miles away, a column of agitated white water on a still day shooting through the air higher than the limes by its side.

The description of its making and the complexity of the technical details which led to the successful outcome of the latest project are set out in Volume XI of Paxton's *Magazine of Botany*. As I am sure this book is by your bed I won't weary you with all that is written therein. But it may be of interest to compare Paxton's achievement with other famous fountains already installed: that at Wilhelmshohe, near Kassel, was then the champion, reaching 190 feet (but by 1844 it was out of order); the next, of 160 feet, was at St Cloud; that at Peterhof played to 120 feet, the old fountain at Chatsworth, now to be superseded, to 94 feet; Versailles could only manage a mere 90 feet.

There had been a fountain at the north end of the Canal since the pond was dug in 1702. It was one of many in the garden at that time and was admired for nearly 150 years for giving the best display, being the highest in this country. Even Walpole had said, *'the great jet d'eau I like'*. Now a new idea came to the Duke – one which had lain dormant since his visit to the embassy at St Petersburg in 1826. The fountain should be the champion of the world and eclipse all others, including the Czar's at Peterhof.

An excuse was soon found to turn his dreams into reality. There was a rumour that Nicholas was to come to England in 1844 and the Duke's dearest wish was that the Emperor should pay a second visit to Chatsworth, where the two men might renew the close friendship they had made in 1816. He wrote in March 1844, *'I am excited and Paxton is frantic about the possibility of Nicholas at Chatsworth.'*

In Paxton he had the right man to create a surprise fit for an Emperor and so the work for the new fountain, which had already begun, was hurried on to be ready in time. A survey of the moor had been made, and hydraulic and pneumatic experiments were carried out to the satisfaction of Paxton and the engineers whose advice he sought. Nothing was left to chance. Although Chatsworth was not short of water the mammoth project would demand a much greater supply, so a new nine-acre reservoir was dug on the flat ground 300 feet above the house and just below the old lake which supplies the Cascade. A conduit two and a half miles across the moor was cut from the Umberley brook near the Chesterfield road which gathered water from springs as it wound its way to the new reservoir. The speed with which all this was carried out must have necessitated an army of men and horses. It makes one wonder how many were employed, where they lodged and many other questions which remain unanswered.

On 18 January 1844 the Duke wrote, *'Paxton on the look out, and made me see without loss of time the wonders he has done in a month. The rocks, the pipes, the waters. The Queens Rock is grand.'* The following day he wrote, *'After lunch in storm and gale I walked up with Paxton to see the spot for the new reservoir, half frightened by the immense work.'* As the date of the Emperor's visit to this country drew near so the pace of work became frenzied and went on all night by the light of flares. In the six winter months the reservoir was completed. The greatest depth at its head is 13 feet

Above Looking east across the Canal and the Emperor Fountain to the beech avenue.

Opposite The Emperor Fountain in the Canal.

Below A lithograph showing the fountain's first display to 264 feet in 1844.

81

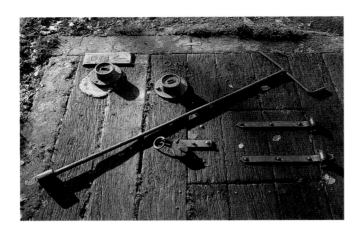

The huge iron key and trap doors covering the valve that opens and closes the Emperor Fountain.

and the average depth is 7 feet. Its banks were lined with stone and 6,200 feet of metal pipes weighing 217 tons were laid. Paxton, the engineer, lovingly described a *'double acting valve, a beautiful piece of mechanism made by Messrs Bury & Kennedy of Liverpool, which takes 5 minutes to fairly open or shut so that the whole may never be let on or off with a shock to the pipes'.*[43]

When the day came for the mighty fountain to perform the Duke was enthralled by what he saw. The jet shot 264 feet heavenwards, far eclipsing any rival. *'Its glorious success — the most majestic object and a new glory to Chatsworth — O Paxton,'* the Duke wrote on 20 July 1844. The bitter disappointment for himself, his engineer/gardener and all concerned when it was known that the Emperor would not have time to make the longed-for visit is not recorded in words, but can be imagined. In spite of the fact that he was never to see it, the fountain was called the Emperor and so it remains today, *'dashing its endless variety to the sky'*. It is still the highest gravity-fed fountain in the world.

Permission was granted for Paxton to dedicate the *Magazine of Botany* which described the making of the fountain to the Czar. In December 1844 a specially bound volume was sent to St Petersburg and, in spite of being wrapped in polite words, the dedication had a faintly hurt tone: *'To His Imperial Majesty The Emperor of Russia, etc, etc, etc. Sire, Having been honoured by a condescending permission, I presume to dedicate to Your Imperial Majesty this ELEVENTH VOLUME OF THE MAGAZINE OF BOTANY; on account of the work being devoted to pursuits on which Your Imperial Majesty has bestowed such liberal encouragement, and because it also contains an account of a Fountain which I have lately constructed at Chatsworth, by the Duke of Devonshire's direction. As this Fountain is the highest in the world, I had ventured humbly to share the hope which he fondly cherished, that its column of water would have first gushed forth when Your Imperial Majesty set foot on the sward of Chatsworth. The compensation he has found is, in bidding it bear the name of "The Emperor". I have the honour to be, Sire, Your Imperial Majesty's Most obedient, humble Servant, Joseph Paxton, Chatsworth December 14th 1844.'*

The Czar of all the Russias thanked the author by sending him the Order of St Anne, some silver gilt beakers and a sable coat – a royal return for the present of a book.

The Emperor Fountain is still turned on and off by hand. An iron valve key, 5 feet long and extremely heavy, lies on a pair of wooden trap doors fastened with a padlock. You must lower the key on to the valve and turn it between ten and twenty-five times depending on the wind. As it rises to its full height the wind can blow it where people stand watching to the delight of the children – until they themselves get a good wetting.

Paxton was one of those rare people who seldom failed in what he set out to do – and he set out to do a lot. Not only was he occupied with practical gardening, forestry, plant introductions, building and engineering, but in 1831 he turned to journalism and was co-editor, with Joseph Harrison, of the *Horticultural Register*. It was an immediate success, meeting a ready audience of people hungry for advice and information on flowers, fruits and vegetables. The articles and letters make fascinating reading today.

There was soon a spirited exchange of words in his new publication, sparked off by an article written by the respected horticulturist, John Claudius Loudon, the owner/editor of *The Gardener's Magazine,* founded in 1826. Perhaps Loudon was peeved by the fact that Paxton, who was still in his twenties, was becoming famous not only as a gardener but also as a journalist and sales of the *Horticultural Register* were exceeding those of his own long-established paper. Loudon went to Chatsworth to see for himself what the young man was up to and was sternly critical of all he found. He called when Paxton was away and later pronounced, *'Chatsworth has always appeared to us as an unsatisfactory place'* (shades of 1760 and Horace Walpole – *'I was never more disappointed than at Chatsworth ...'*).[44]

Loudon went on to make wild suggestions for improving the waterworks by altering the course of the river. *'We believe the river might be turned off at a sufficiently high point and led along the sides of the hills.'* His ideas were pure fantasy and he realises he may have gone too far: *'we are aware of the risk of misconception which we incur by offering these hints without the illustration of a sketch.'*

Then he had a go at the flower garden, condemning the new gravel walks. In the kitchen garden he complains of a long bed of ornamental plants bordered by turf serrated on the edges. *'Nothing of this sort ought, in our opinion, ever to be introduced in such a kitchen garden; we would as soon introduce a plot of cabbages in the newly formed parterre of the house.'*

This was too much for Paxton, who wrote a long and detailed reply to Loudon in Vol. I of his *Horticultural Register*. He concluded: *'I hope you will continue to criticise public gardens: this is quite a different affair; but in England, every man's house being his castle, whether he chooses to live upon salt and water, or ornament his window with a bouquet of cabbages, no one, we conceive, has any business with it.'*

A few years later the feud was forgotten and they wrote for each other's publications. When Loudon died in poverty it was Paxton who raised money to help his widow.

I wish the protagonists could have seen the garden I visited a few years ago in Washington DC. It belonged to the doyenne of taste in that town. Her plot of cabbages without and bouquets of cabbages within were the stars of the show.

So great was Paxton's energy that it could not be confined by the Cavendish properties. He became famous as the architect of the Crystal Palace which housed the Great Exhibition of 1851, for which he was knighted; he also became a director of railway companies and MP for Coventry from 1854 to his death in 1865. Yet he was still indispensable to the Duke, to whom he remained a faithful servant and friend.

The Bachelor Duke's own contribution to horticulture and silviculture in England is incalculable. He supported the London shows of the Royal Horticultural Society and served as its president for twenty years from 1838 till his death. From the day he confessed to being *'bit by gardening'* he lavished vast sums on plants. The owners of the famous nursery gardens in and around London must have rubbed their hands in anticipation when he arrived, like an art dealer who spots a representative of the Getty Museum at his door. The account books show that the annual expenditure on plants reached a maximum of £1,194 in 1841 when they were buying for the Great Conservatory. It was nearly as large a sum for many years.

The combination of a rich and innovative owner and a clever, energetic and practical leader of men who could turn his hand to anything and was also a skilled horticulturist came at the right time. The spirit of confidence in the nineteenth century coincided with the heady excitement of plant-hunting expeditions to hitherto unexplored jungles and mountains all over the world, as well as new technology and materials for building and engineering – undreamed of revelations in both spheres which inspired our two heroes.

One of the results of their enthusiasm was the number of plants named after the Cavendish family and their gardener. Paxton's *Magazine of Botany* (1834–49) illustrates some of them. They shared a particular passion for orchids and, in addition to the *Dendrobium devonianum*, other orchids named after them included *Oncidium cavendishianum*, *Cymbidium devonianum*, *Cattleya* × *devoniana*, *Galeandra devoniana*, *Stanhopea devoniensis* (now *S. hernandezii*), *Burlingtonia rigida* (now *Rodriquezia rigida*), *Dendrobium paxtonii* (now *D. chrysanthum*) and the

Jim Link, turning on the fountain: 10 to 25 turns are required, depending on the wind, till the water reaches the required height.

Galeandra devonianum, as illustrated in Paxton's *Magazine of Botany*.

Dendrobium devonianum, as illustrated in Paxton's *Magazine of Botany*.

genus *Paxtonia* (now *Spathoglottis*). Devonshire's family name was also commemorated in such plants as the water lily *Nymphaea* 'Devoniensis', the ivy *Hedera helix* 'Cavendishii', the carnation *Dianthus* 'Duke of Devonshire' and the apple *Malus* 'Duke of Devonshire'. The description of this is not appetising: 'Skin — very dry, dull green becoming yellow, covered with patchy and netted grey-brown russet spreading over the cheeks. Sometimes finely scaled. Eyes — slightly to half open.' Nevertheless this curious apple is still available from a few specialist nurseries.

Under the Duke's patronage and Paxton's direction, and with the services of a staff of whom many went on to be head gardeners elsewhere, Chatsworth had become the most famous garden in England. Water, rocks and glass had been used to make their various stunning effects. In the greenhouses and out of doors trees, flowers and fruit were grown to perfection. The combination of all these was unique. Medals were won for pineapples, peaches, nectarines, figs, melons and the dwarf banana, *Musa acuminata* 'Cavendishii'. The orchid houses set a fashion and Paxton's revolutionary methods of growing them became the accepted way for amateurs and professionals alike. The Pinetum and Arboretum were copied by others who had enough space and so the flattering imitation multiplied.

With Paxton, the Duke threw unlimited enthusiasm, money and skill into every branch of the science and practice, and helped to popularise it by welcoming every Tom, Dick and Harry to see what was going on at Chatsworth as no one has done before or since.

This was one of the differences between Chatsworth and other great nineteenth-century gardens — all were welcome to come and see. And all came. The crowds arrived regularly and in ever-increasing numbers from Derby, Sheffield and as far away as Lincoln. When the railway reached Rowsley — three miles away — in the summer of 1849 about 80,000 people visited the house and garden, and so it was every year from then on. *'The humblest individual is not only shown the whole but the Duke has expressly ordered the waterworks to be played for everyone without exception'.*[45] There was no charge. The indoor servants acted as guides in the house, while the gardeners showed people round their domain.

This duty was called 'partying' by the gardener/diarist Robert Aughtie, on 31 July 1848. *'A large party came from Sheffield — went partying — showed a party of nine round, who gave me only seven pence at which I was vexed — attended a meeting at the girls school room — the Bishop of Madras was to have been there but was prevented — Mr Ellison lectured on the Missionaries — had some talk about the lodger with Mrs Wallace — it was settled that I was to stop.'*[46] This entry covers a day in village life which, with the star speaker failing to turn up and the lecture on missionaries turned into flower arranging, could have been written today.

The excitement of an outing on the new-fangled train is caught by the reporter of the *Derbyshire Courier* (an account kept by Robert Aughtie in his diary). This party was organised by a keen temperance worker from Sheffield called Thomas Cook. His son, also Thomas Cook, went on to win fame and fortune in the same line of business — and not only for teetotallers. *'June 30th 1849 — Last Tuesday, being the day appointed for the great pleasure trip and temperance gathering in Chatsworth park — as early as five o'clock the principal streets leading to the Midland station were thronged by people of all descriptions, eagerly making their way to the train, which was about to convey them to scenes of which they had heard so much but which few of them had seen. After having seen the main body fairly on the rails, we turned to another party of excursionists (not teetotallers) bound for the same scenes, by a different route, choosing the road to Baslow, and availing themselves of hired vehicles of every description. We have been in Doncaster on the morning of the great St Leger day, when the monstrous cavalcade has begun to move on towards the course, but never saw anything to equal the sight which presented itself on the morning of Tuesday last, in South street and Sheffield Moor, the whole street being from one end to the other, one complete line of carriages, carts, cabs, cars and omnibuses. No matter how or in what way they got off every one seemed in the highest spirits as they proceeded en route to the hills of Derbyshire. We again return to our friends the teetotallers, who had by this time arrived safely at the Rowsley station,[where] omnibuses and conveyances of all sorts were in waiting, which were soon filled; and, fortunately, many were inclined to walk the short distance of three miles. The pedestrians having arrived within sight of Chatsworth House, a scene presented itself, of which it is difficult to convey any idea — the great park and grounds in front of the house being one complete mass of people, all arrayed in their holiday attire, not a few amongst the number having been elegantly fitted out — as the shapes and fashion of their vestments manifested — at Moses and Son's establishment, to the no small admiration and astonishment of the country folks, who had never before seen such a gay and fashionable assemblage. Through the condescension and kindness of the noble Duke of Devonshire, the excursionists were allowed to go through the magnificent rooms of the palace, and they were permitted to visit the splendid gardens and pleasure grounds. 'Between 4,000 and 5,000 persons were at one time, it is believed, promenading in the park, in the palace, and in the pleasure-grounds of Chatsworth!'*

Cymbidium devonianum, as illustrated in Paxton's *Magazine of Botany*.

The 6th Duke moved heaven and earth to bring the railway closer than Rowsley, to come through the park in fact. This seems as strange now as it would be to try to persuade the authorities to bring the M1 along the same route. But the Duke was a man who wanted to modernise for the prosperity of all, and rail transport was the key.

In 1849 Paxton had managed to get the track extended from Ambergate to Rowsley (the 'Chatsworth Line' the locals called it), and now it was to progress to Manchester. Should it run along the Wye valley past Haddon Hall or follow the River Derwent via Chatsworth to Baslow? The Duke of Rutland did not fancy the 'iron courser' tearing by his garden at Haddon, but the Duke of Devonshire took the opposite view and gave £50,000 to the project, which he thought would be *'to the great public advantage'*, and told them they could go where they liked through his park.

George Stephenson planned a tunnel under Park Wood, a few hundred yards from the house, which would emerge at Buston where Baslow Station would be built. Then the Duke of Rutland, attracted by the promise of generous compensation for disturbance, suddenly changed his mind and began lobbying for the Haddon route. The issue was debated in Parliament and a House of Lords committee voted against the Chatsworth way. Devonshire withdrew his £50,000 and it was not till 1863 that the trains went through to Manchester. It was a close-run thing. How different would the park have been and how changed the view from the house and garden had the trains been pounding along a line through Brown's tranquil landscape.

The fulsome accounts of the pleasure to be found here by the newspapers of the day make strange reading to people used to the sarcasm of 1990s reporting. But there is no doubt that the house and garden must have seemed like fairyland, a vision of another world, to day trippers from the neighbouring industrial towns, the crowded smoking cities of steel foundries and noisy textile factories. They came in their thousands to see the latest additions to an already remarkable place.

Dendrobium paxtonii (now *D. chrysanthum*), as illustrated in Paxton's *Magazine of Botany*.

The seed of affection for Chatsworth was sown in many families and it became the place to go for a day out for anyone seeking peace and beauty. The tradition continues and the great-great-great-grandchildren of those early sightseers still come, now in their BMWs.

When the Bachelor Duke died in 1858 Paxton arranged every detail of his late master's funeral. After the last mourner had left he knew he was no longer needed and, with his innate tact, stayed not a day longer but left Derbyshire for ever.

'We have to be economical'

The 7th, 8th, 9th and 10th Dukes

1858—1950

Previous pages The Rose Garden made by my mother-in-law in 1939 in front of the 1st Duke's greenhouse. In the nineteenth century it was known as the French Garden. The Bachelor Duke removed the pillars and the seventeenth-century stone busts and urns from the inner court in the house and placed them here.

Below An illustration in *The Graphic* on 28 December 1872 shows the gentlemen in the Orangery after dinner sitting in cane chairs, smoking. The Prince of Wales is staring into the middle distance, bored to death by another guest who seems to be trying to get his attention.

Opposite above An English, nineteenth-century marble figure of Paris after the Antique. It was one of the Bachelor Duke's many purchases of statuary.

Opposite below The West Front, floodlit as it is every night.

The 7th Duke, William Cavendish (1808–91), the Bachelor Duke's cousin, being by nature shy and scholarly, was not interested in the glittering show that Chatsworth had become. He was Chancellor of London University at the age of twenty-eight and later Chancellor of Cambridge University, a mathematician and a Fellow of the Royal Society. As a widower, without his beloved Blanche, the last thing he wanted was to entertain at Chatsworth. The extravagances of his predecessor weighed heavily on him. The Bachelor Duke had created something extraordinary, but at an immense cost, and he had died owing a great deal of money. The new Duke had to act swiftly to pay his cousin's debts. He took his responsibilities as a landowner as seriously as he took everything in life, and the house and garden remained open to the public. Quantities of 'Black Hamburgh' and 'Madresfield Court' grapes and other fruit were sent to local hospitals, where they '*effected more good, quietly, feelingly and unostentatiously than would be by the gift of five times their value in money*',[47] but the garden did little more than just tick over. In spite of economies, expenditure on the woodwork, glazing and paint of the innumerable glasshouses was a large annual item and although the amount spent on plants, seeds and shrubs every year was less than half that of the great years under the 6th Duke, it was still about £500, a substantial sum.

Making sure that all was well in the garden seemed to be a duty rather than a pleasure for its owner and was fitted in with the business of running his huge estates and a number of industrial projects. '*I had time to go over the gardens before I left Chatsworth. Much is coming into flower particularly the orchid houses*,' he recorded in his diary on 14 February 1872. The following year he did allow himself to be pleased with what he found. '*There are not much signs of spring here but the orchid houses are in great beauty. The fine plants of Camellia reticulata in the Portland Walk are in great perfection*.' Usually the only guests in the house were family or close friends, so it was quite an event when, in December 1872, the Prince and Princess of Wales spent three nights here. One gets the impression that the only reason they came was because Chatsworth was a convenient lodging after a long round of royal duties in Derby and it was indicated that the Duke, as Lord Lieutenant of the county, should be their host. The West Front and Cascade were illuminated for their arrival, but it was a still, foggy night and smoke descended from the flares and fireworks and hid everything. It penetrated the hall, which was '*full of sulphur ... and set us coughing*', wrote Lady Frederick Cavendish[48] in her diary. She noticed that someone had tried hard with the plants to decorate the dining room. '*Dinner very fine, with feathery cocos palm springing out of the table in the midst and overshadowing us*.' There was little joy in the conventional entertainments arranged for the guests. Lady Frederick described a '*rather ponderous and oppressive big County ball*' in a hot and dusty room. But things looked up at supper, which was '*a lovely and peculiar sight in the Sculpture Gallery, carpeted with red cloth and adorned with great bananas, ferns, palms etc. The great granite basin filled with green, a slender palm in the middle and stiff white hyacinths blooming round the palm, reminded me somehow of the ancient pictures of the Virgin's tomb filled with flowers*.' Lady Frederick was quite often reminded of a sad scene from the Bible, but this one seems to have set the tone for the Royal visit.

The entry in the Duke's diary for 21 December sums up his feelings: '*I am not sorry that the visit of the Prince and Princess is over*.' From forty people staying in the house the company was reduced to twelve that day and the unwilling but dutiful host was mightily relieved.

The number of people visiting the house and the garden every summer continued to grow. In 1884 a record was reached when 3,500 people toured the house on the Tuesday of Whit week. What they could have seen but ceilings and each other I do not know, but the crowds were undeterred and arrived in their thousands to be shown round for no charge, just as they had been in the late Duke's time.

The eldest son of the serious, studious William was Spencer Compton, called Cavendish by his father, Cav by contemporaries, and Uncle Cav by his nephews and nieces. He was fifty-eight when he succeeded as the 8th Duke in 1891. He had already had a long career in politics, having been an MP since he was twenty-four, held various Cabinet posts and led the Liberal Party from 1875 to 1886. The Queen asked him to form a Government three times — in 1880, 1886 and 1887 — and each time he stood aside for another.

A few months after his father died he married the widowed Duchess of Manchester, born Louise von Alten, with whom he had had a long love affair. There had been no Duchess of Devonshire at Chatsworth for eighty years and although neither of them was young, the place came to life again under the new regime.

One of the first things they did was to harness Chatsworth's natural water supply to provide electrical power for the house. Three Gilbert Gilkes and Gordon Vortex turbines were installed in 1893 in a building hidden at the south end of the West Garden. Chatsworth was one of the first big houses to make its own electricity, following the example of Hatfield House, Hertfordshire, a few years earlier. Water had always been a force for beauty here, but now it became a force for use as well. How Paxton would have revelled in the new

Above The table laden with flowers for a dinner party in 1897. *Below and opposite above* Table decorations in our dining room today: camellias in a silver dish; and pelargoniums crammed into silver vases.

Opposite below Calanthe orchids in the Blue Drawing Room which remain there for six winter weeks.

technology which made that free and renewable element work to such advantage. For forty-three years the flow of water from the hills above the house did its job until, in 1936, it was decided to link the house with the National Grid. The turbines were forgotten, my mother-in-law took the glass accumulator cells from the turbine house for flower vases, rhododendrons pushed the roof in and all was quiet in the building that had caused so much excitement.

(In 1986 John Oliver, then Assistant Comptroller, looked at the electricity bills at Chatsworth and remembered the turbine house. He persuaded Andrew to let him start it up again. Nearly a hundred years after it was first built, with new turbines from the same firm that the originals came from, it roars away again, when the rainfall allows, and provides the majority of our power needs during the winter months. A 1920s telephone, the kind which looks like a black daffodil, and a little fireplace are still there. All this is of great interest to people who join our 'Behind the Scenes' tours; it is a place of wonder, a mixture of ancient and modern, and a demonstration of man's ingenuity in making nature work for him.)

Louise was the very pattern of a political hostess, enjoying it all herself and indulging her talent for entertaining, which reached its zenith when Edward VII came to the throne. Hostesses vied with one another, going to great lengths to please the monarch and his delightful Queen. There are formal photographs of the King at Chatsworth on his annual visits, getting ever stouter as the years went by.

The November and December shooting parties meant the hot houses coming back into their own, producing exotic fruit and flowers to be eaten and admired, and in 1900 the Great Conservatory was put into good order for the last time. The decorations in the house for these winter festivities reached a peak of extravagance. The dining table for forty carried different flowers every night and as the guests stayed for up to a week in those days the greenhouse men had to make a huge effort. There was a 'decorator' on the garden staff and it was he who disposed the palms, ferns and orchids in the library and drawing rooms, passages and bedrooms, as well as in the dining room, to delight the company.

Today Ian Webster is the latest of a long line of decorators. He combines this role with being the glasshouse foreman. His is a skill I admire greatly as I am incapable of arranging flowers. In one room we have copied my sister Nancy. When she lived in Versailles she put her flowers together on a table instead of dotting vases and pots round the room. In the Blue Drawing Room they are all on one table under the enormous painting of *The Acheson Sisters* by John Singer Sargent. The flowers here are always blue and white – other colours do not seem to look right, but all shades of blue seem to 'go' satisfactorily. The exception to this rule is the pink and white calanthe orchids which occupy the table at Christmas and remain there for six weeks. They are not watered during this time, so they do not need saucers under their pots, but they do need dusting by the end of January. Nancy Lancaster, the creator of the most enviable gardens I have known, hated orchids. She thought them ugly, and more annoying because they last so long. I can understand her dislike of the solidly vulgar cymbidiums, but calanthes are another matter and I can't help wondering if she had ever seen them.

Ian is a master at dining-table decoration, often using little trees or big flowers. He brings in mop-headed *Lavandula dentata* or small standard hollies in pots which he covers with moss. In July he puts rambling roses in narrow four-feet-tall Edwardian glass vases, allowing their

Above The Weather Station
on the Salisbury lawns.
Below Recent entries in the
Weather Book.
Bottom The crystal ball which
measures the hours of sunshine
at Chatsworth.

WEATHER			
B denotes Blue Sky		P denotes Showery	

Chatsworth Weather Reports

Month ...... MARCH
Year 1999

Readings of the Barometer and Thermometer and Remar

Date	BAR	THERMOMETER			WIND
		MAX.	MIN.	7.30 a.m.	Direction at 7.30 a.m.
1	29·18	53	42	50	WSW
2	29·22	53	45	51	SW
3	28·58	48	42	44	SW

long stems to flop about as they do when they are growing. In both cases diners can see each other across the table. In November pink and white cyclamen flowers or 'Rayonnante' chrysanthemums are picked and stuffed into silver bowls; in April narcissus get the same treatment, as do azaleas in May, red roses in July and dahlias in September. At Christmas hollies and sprigs of mistletoe cover big plates. Bay trees are also brought indoors at Christmas and tangerines are fixed on to them with wires – a ruse to pretend they are orange trees. This strange idea is not a recent invention but is traditional here.

A speciality at Chatsworth is the myrtle, *Myrtus communis* subsp. *tarentina*. These too are clipped into mop-heads – a nail-scissor job. The dark green leaves are small and dense, a foil for the exuberant decoration in the dining room, where there is a lot of gilding. The *Daily Telegraph* described the way that they were used when King George V and Queen Mary came to stay in 1933. *'Last night the mansion at Chatsworth was the scene of pre-war splendour in honour of the Royal visit. Gold plate was used for the Duchess of Devonshire's dinner party, the most brilliant of the series she has planned. On this occasion the old-world myrtles which she is using throughout her home were the sole decoration on the banqueting table. On the centre of the table stood a huge gold bowl of fruit.'* Many myrtles were lost in 1990 when a branch of a cedar crashed through the glass of their house after a heavy snowfall, but they are growing again in their slow way.

Lapageria rosea (and its varieties 'White Cloud' and 'Flesh Pink'), the national flower of Chile, is also brought inside. It has narrow bell-shaped flowers that naturally hang down, but they are set pointing upwards in a plate of scented geranium leaves. Usually such cavalier treatment of nature, turning things upside down, does not succeed but in the case of lapageria I think it does. White, pink or red, the flowers are made, apparently, of thick wax and you have to touch them to understand that they are real.

The 8th Duke was not in the least interested in domestic matters. He had no idea who was staying in the house and was once heard to say, *'I wish I knew who my guests are.'* He left all the arrangements to Louise, a past mistress of cheerful display. But he must have been vaguely aware that there was something special about what was grown in the glasshouses because in 1892 he wrote to Joseph Chamberlain, then Secretary for the Colonies, who was planning a visit when the host could not be at home, *'I imagine from your letter that you would prefer seeing Chatsworth as an ordinary tourist, but if you would like to see anything which is not usually shown, orchids for instance, and will send me a wire, I will write or telegraph at once.'*[49]

According to the 1905 list of greenhouses, the Kitchen Garden must have been more like a glass village than the accepted idea for such a piece of ground with a few rows of vegetables and soft fruits. Thirty-three glazed buildings were described separately as 'fruit' and 'plants' plus the Lily House, a propagating house and thirteen others, all covering 30,239 square feet, or just under seven-tenths of an acre. In the Pleasure Grounds (i.e. the garden proper) 20,414 square feet, or just under half an acre, was covered in glass. Add the Great Conservatory of three-quarters of an acre and you have a grand total of about two acres of greenhouses.

Today there are some 25,000 square feet under glass, where semi-hardy and tender plants prosper. What the Bachelor Duke called *'the eternal calm of the greenhouse'* offers an escape from some of the drawbacks of the harsh climate. My mother-in-law loved the people here but she did not love the climate, saying that the lack of sunshine made living in Derbyshire like living in the bottom of a well. Chatsworth is high up in the middle of England; its situation is fully exposed to the west wind, and there is always a cracking frost in May. To add to the difficulties of gardening here, a lot of the ground is 'made-up' – man-made hills and levels which are not appreciated by plants, even after two or three hundred years. For these reasons Chatsworth is not a plantsman's garden.

The daily fluctuations in the weather at Chatsworth have been noted more or less continuously since the eighteenth century. Keeping the records is one of the duties of the Head Gardener. The strict rules that applied to a Head Gardener are recorded in a letter confirming the appointment of Mr Frank Jennings in the post on 15 August 1906. It states that no apprentices could be taken on any account, no special expenses could to be incurred without permission and no discount or commission taken from tradesmen, but that house, coals, firing and gas would be free. Mr Jennings's wages were to be £140 per year rising to £180. The last condition of employment was that meteorological observations were '*to be taken every day and carefully noted in a book kept for the purpose*'.

No doubt an official meteorological station would consider our methods in arriving at the figures to be very amateur, but they are valuable in that they compare like with like. After the last war Andrew, to his delight, discovered that there had been no break in the records and that they were up to date. The Weather Book is kept in the dining room now and a daily note of rainfall, hours of sunshine, etc. arrives every morning.

We know that the English are obsessed with the weather and the diarists among the Devonshires were no exceptions. The 7th Duke started every entry with the state of the weather, usually too dull to quote, but sometimes, as on 23 November 1873, we are woken up by a comment such as '*it blew very hard last night and the early part of today. A good deal of damage has been done to the large conservatory and a few trees have been blown down or damaged.*' The 8th Duke was too sleepy to keep a diary, but the 9th Duke never failed to record the weather. In 1910 he wrote, '*Violent thunderstorm. Mother Hubbard dropped dead.*' Mother Hubbard was a loved Shire mare.

To indulge this interest there has been a 'weather station' on the Salisbury lawns for many years. The rain gauge is measured and emptied every day and there is an ingenious method for recording the hours of sunshine: a fortune teller's crystal ball is mounted on a curved iron frame and paper with the hours printed on it is inserted behind the crystal. When the sun shines through the glass it burns the paper so that you can read when and for how long the sun has been out by the singe marks.

The average annual rainfall for the forty-nine years between 1761 and 1810 was 28.4 inches; the wettest year was 1768, with 39.9 inches, and the driest was 1780,with 19.4 inches. During the last forty-nine years from 1949 to 1998 the average was 32.97 inches; the wettest year was 1981, when 41.59 inches fell, and the driest was 1975, with 24.72 inches. Chatsworth has got damper but warmer. Gone are the bitterly cold winters when there was no let-up from frost for several weeks, as in 1940, 1947 and 1963. Instead we have to suffer cold and rain in April and May, which is not conducive to successful gardening.

After the death of his childless uncle in 1908, Victor Christian William became 9th Duke of Devonshire. He immediately made what was perhaps an overdue but none the less revolutionary change at Chatsworth: for the first time a charge of one shilling was made to see round the house and garden. The money went to local hospitals, which in those days were dependent on public support. It was not until 1949 that the entrance money helped to maintain what people came to see.

Above, from top The maze in March; on a frosty morning in May; and later in the summer.

Above The avenue to Blanche's Vase after a snowstorm.

Below The Wellington Rock frozen, with yard-long icicles.

At the age of twenty-three, when he was returned unopposed as MP for West Derbyshire in 1891, Victor had become the youngest member of the House of Commons. He remained interested in politics all his life and was Secretary of State for the Colonies from 1922 to 1925. In 1892 he had married Lady Evelyn Fitzmaurice and their country home was Holker Hall in Lancashire. They and their children adored the place, and were very unhappy when they had to move to Chatsworth and Holker passed to the new Duke's brother, Lord Richard Cavendish, his wife Lady Moyra and their growing family.

The sorrow of a twelve-year-old child leaving everything she knew and loved was described by their eldest daughter Maud. *'We scarcely knew Uncle Cav ... His death brought a complete upheaval in our lives and a change (in our opinion) definitely for the worse, because it meant leaving Holker ... We spent the Easter holidays [of 1908] there for the last time and I had my twelfth birthday, with my last wreath of Holker primroses. It was a very sad time saying goodbye to our little gardens, to the Farm, to our favourite keeper who introduced us to so many birds, and to the woods we loved so much. I remember the drive to the Station, tears streaming down all our faces, my father's included. From that day we never really felt we had a home, as we had far too many. It was useless to try and garden, as we were never in the same place when the seeds or bulbs we have planted appeared above ground.'*[50]

The new Duchess, known to us as Granny Evie, was very interested in gardening but can have had little time to indulge herself in it. A family of seven children, a politician husband who had to live a large part of the year in London and the responsibility for the housekeeping of five other houses and gardens overtook time for new schemes for Chatsworth. She just accepted it as it was and let it all run along the accustomed lines.

The Devonshires led a nomadic existence, forever packing and travelling from one big house to another. Maud described how their year was divided: *'Early in January we went to Lismore until the end of the Easter holiday.'* This meant children, nanny, governess, nursery maids, valet, lady's maid, ponies and dogs boarding a special train to catch the boat for Ireland. *'Then London until mid-July, with a break at Whitsuntide, when we generally went to Chatsworth. In July we went to Eastbourne, to Compton Place, a lovely house in a large garden ... After Eastbourne we spent a few days at Chatsworth before the great exodus to Bolton. We spent three or four weeks there, followed by a month or more at Hardwick, returning to Chatsworth until after the New Year.'*[51] So they only spent about three months of the year at Chatsworth, mostly in the winter.

This relentless routine was followed religiously until 1916 when, after much deliberation, the Duke accepted the appointment as Governor General of Canada, which meant a five-year absence from home. Meanwhile, at Chatsworth as everywhere else, the young men joined up following the outbreak of the First World War of 1914–18, and only a few boys and old men were left to look after the garden. It deteriorated fast. Only the most necessary maintenance was carried out and the negative effect was felt long after the peace was signed. In 1917 a list of the garden staff, their ages and length of service was sent to the Devonshires in Canada. The twenty men were all aged forty-three or over, too old for military service. Walter Brightmore, aged sixty-one, had fifty-two years' service – so he must have started work when he was nine. Two were described as *'night men'* and one as *'tomato grower'*. At the bottom of the page, almost as an afterthought, the clerk added *'5 boys and 4 girls. The 2 oldest boys will join up next year. These are most useful and the girls for packing etc.'*

The glasshouses were one more casualty of the war. There is an entry in Victor's diary for 14 January 1920 which shows that the Bachelor Duke's extravagances of another age had no place in the hard times which had arrived. *'Telegram from Burke* [Roland Burke was Head Agent for the Duke's estates based at Chatsworth] *saying there was an offer of £550 for the Kitchen*

Garden greenhouses. Wired acceptance. They will be a good riddance.'

Burke replied: 'The price provided for cash down before anything was touched, and includes all the Greenhouses together with all wrought iron pipes and so forth, but excepting all lead pipes, paving blocks and the brick or stone masonry. The Purchaser is to clear the whole lot and to take away both good and bad within 3 months.

'After receiving the final offer of £550, I made a very careful examination of the whole of the Houses, and came to the conclusion that serious deterioration had taken place during the period of the War, and considerable expenditure would be necessary in the way of painting and general repairs if the Houses are to be used again. There are, of course, some Houses which have been put up within the last 15 years which are in good order, but even these require paint immediately, but a large quantity of the glass is in a thoroughly delapidated condition and is practically worth nothing at all, as the labour in these items is a very serious matter.

Above Forty-six gardeners including the proverbial garden-boys in front of the Great Conservatory in c.1890.

'Then, looking at the question from the other point, it seemed to me, since you had expressed the definite opinion and wish that the Kitchen Gardens should be discontinued, it is no good attempting to make use of any of these Houses again, and if they are to be sold it is useless waiting until further deterioration takes place. The fruit trees, themselves, have, of course, suffered considerably by the wet continually dripping in, and although, of course, some of the Vines are in good condition, something must be sacrificed, and I really think that the price which has been obtained is, on the whole, quite as much as can be expected.

'I have got cash down for the purchase and the dismantling will proceed immediately.'

Victor was in England to see how things were going in 1920. The future looked dim. In his diary on 1 April 1920 he noted, 'Burke came in the morning & we had a long talk. Wages. Labour. Conditions generally are so changed from all that [I knew that] I shall take some time to pick them up. In the afternoon we walked to the Kitchen Garden. Melancholy scene ... Had another look at the Pleasure Ground. It is not easy to see light.' He seemed puzzled as to how Chatsworth and all that went with it should be run under such changed circumstances. Victor felt he now had no alternative but to order the destruction of the Great Conservatory.

I have often wondered whether he and Granny Evie found the decision to destroy their own crystal palace a difficult one to make. There is no mention of it in the Duke's diary, but probably the worry of its upkeep had become so great that it outweighed any regret they may have had.

In January 1920 Burke had written to the Duke: 'From the same purchaser [as for the kitchen garden greenhouses] I have received an offer of £600 for the Great House [Great Conservatory]. The price includes the whole fabric with the exception of the stone masonry of the walls, and including the whole of the piping (with the exception of 400 ft and all the lead pipes which I have reserved). It also includes the risk of taking the House down. I have carefully gone into the whole question and consider that the price is as much as can be expected to be got, although it sounds a small sum. There are various points, however, to be taken into consideration:—

'1. That the glass is of practically no value as it is all of such narrow width, being only 6 inches wide.

2. *The whole structure is of wood construction, most of which is in an extremely rotten condition and of practically no value except for firewood.*

3. *There is considerable risk in taking the building down, and it will mean very costly scaffolding, and probably heavy insurance of the men employed.*

4. *The cost of the labour entailed will be extremely heavy, and further, there will be heavy outlay in carting away as it is very inconveniently situated.*

Generally the offer of £600 has been made almost entirely for the value of the hot water pipes in the building.

I should be glad if you would kindly Cable your wishes on this very important question. Possibly you may prefer to have it held over till your return, as I can quite appreciate it is a difficult question to decide upon. I am convinced, however, that the House will have to be pulled down in the more or less near future. The building is in a very bad state, as of course there has been no painting done for some considerable time, and serious deterioration is taking place very fast. Proper painting both outside and in, and considerable repairs to both glass and wood are necessary if the building is to remain up. I have had these points carefully gone into, and estimate that, at present prices, this could not be done under £2500.'

The fateful decision was made and on 25 May 1920 Burke reported to the Duke: *'Last Saturday, Mr White, the purchaser, tried to complete the demolition of the House by high explosive. Every arrangement was made to fire off the charges that afternoon, but it was midnight before he had got all completed, and it was then decided to defer the whole explosion until yesterday, Monday. Unfortunately, however, the newspapers had got a full account of the whole of the explosion written out, which forthwith appeared in yesterday's papers, saying that the explosion was terrific, was heard for some miles, and some billion pieces of glass were scattered about the country, and that the Great House was now no more!! However, we did have a try to blow it up yesterday: Charlie Markham* [Paxton's grandson] *came over and brought various apparatus, and we had about seven or eight attempts, and although very high charges were used, it had not the slightest effect on the building, the roof remaining quite stationary. The most extraordinary thing about it was that really very little glass was broken in the roof. I am feeling quite guilty in having persuaded you to take the building down, as if it can stand the terrific charges exploded beneath it, I believe it would have stood up for many years! As I write this I have heard renewed attempts to blow it down, and so I hope I may report something later. We had a Cinema man there yesterday, and if the films are anything like satisfactory I am going to send them out to you.'* He added a postscript: *'Another heavy charge Tues. evening completed the work. The whole roof falling in.'*

Perhaps the Great Conservatory was doomed anyway, as taxes were rising and the spectre of death duties had to be reckoned with. To keep it going would have been a huge extravagance in labour, fuel and maintenance, and neither Victor nor Granny Evie was extravagant.

For those who had known it in its glory it was a tragedy and for us who have lived through the 1950s and '60s it was a foretaste of the destruction to come of so many wonderful buildings in this country. The poignancy of its end after repeated explosions was described by a contemporary writer. *'I stood in the rain today, in a tree-girt enclosure, looking long and sadly at a dismal expanse of debris stretching away from my feet to where tall trees swayed down as if to hide the spectacle. Great iron pillars snapped in several pieces littered the ground. Thick baulks of timber, split and shivered, sprawled about. Over the turf was spread a glittering carpet of broken glass, some of which has frosted the long strips of iron lattice work included in this motley company. A stone ornamented doorway stood isolated at one end of the mass. At intervals were gaunt iron columns, apparently firmly erect, and along one side of the enclosure was a curving glass screen, extending the entire length of the open space, and its top was jagged. Out of the litter two withered palm trees raised their forlorn heads; a cluster of ferns sprang freshly-green from a giant stalk. But elsewhere the falling beams and columns had borne down into the earth the numerous trees and*

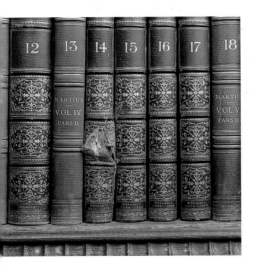

Below A curious reminder of the repeated explosions needed to destroy the glasshouse: a piece of iron was blown through the air and descended into the courtyard of the house with enough force to break a window and embed itself in the binding of a volume of Martius' *Flora Braziliensis*. The damaged book has not been moved and there is a plaque above it to explain the hole.

Opposite This was the dismal scene after the repeated explosions had begun to demolish the Bachelor Duke's pride and joy, the Great Conservatory. The plants had died of cold and neglect during the First World War of 1914–18 and the 9th Duke decided such an extravagance had no place in post-war austerity.

plants. My companion, an old retainer, exclaimed, "A national calamity!" I agreed, for this vast heap of broken glass and metal was all that remained of the proud conservatory of Chatsworth.'[52] The wonder of the Peak District had lasted only eighty years. An ironic touch was that it was Paxton's grandson who had the miserable job of levelling his grandfather's *chef-d'oeuvre*.

The Great Conservatory Garden

There is little left now to remind you of Paxton's masterpiece. A distinct hump in the retaining wall of the bank to the north-west of the site marks the tunnel where the coal trucks ran on their way to the furnaces. The only signs of the great building itself are the sandstone foundation walls which survive and give an indication of the scale. Diagonal flights of steps at the four corners lead to the surrounding banks and thence over the two stoutly built arches across the drive at the north and south ends.

The Conservatory left a big plot to be tidied up and planned anew. Granny Evie planted a double row of crab apples on the lawn surrounding the walls in the 1920s. We thought them out of scale with their surroundings, and cut them down. Imagine my feelings when the man wielding the axe told me that it was he who had planted them thirty years earlier.

In the 1920s flower beds were laid out at each end within the remaining walls of the great building, with paths through and round them. The planting has changed but the beds remain. We have filled them with autumn flowers at the north end: dahlias, Michaelmas daisies and Japanese anemones — all reds, blues and sugar pinks with no hint of orange. The Michaelmas daisies have a sadly brief flowering time as they are reluctant to come out before mid-September and there is often an early frost which blackens them, but they give a splendid show, and are covered in bees and butterflies. Long before the autumn plants begin to flower tree peonies (*Paeonia suffruticosa*), my favourites, lead you to the maze. The blowsy pink 'Duchess of Marlborough' and the huge white 'Mrs William Kelway', with flowers a foot across and petals like crumpled silk, smell of summer.

The south end is all lupins. An advantage of a having very big garden is being able to give an area to a really good show of one kind of flower and then forget it when it is over. The lupins are a case in point. When at their best they are showstoppers, cameras come out and for a couple of weeks they are supreme. It is seldom that a gardener can look at his work with complete satisfaction, but here, at the south end of the maze, I have seen it happen.

The little trees of mop-headed acacias (*Robinia pseudoacacia* 'Umbraculifera') among the flowers in both the north and south beds give height and their leaves remain pale spring-green till autumn. Their disadvantage is being so brittle. A snowfall means broken branches.

In between the beds two hard tennis courts were laid. Andrew remembers changing into white flannels in the dark recesses on either side of the entrance arches. Except to those who love playing tennis, the courts were not beautiful. Luckily the old pipes underneath soon turned the surface into hills and dales which did not help the game. So once again the use of the space was changed and in 1962 we planted a maze.

Below Clipping the yew maze. This annual task takes four men 7–10 days in August. In the middle of the maze is a weeping pear tree (*Pyrus salicifolia* 'Pendula'). The Lawson cypress trees in the background were planted by Paxton when the Great Conservatory was built.

Opposite, above and below The tennis courts and flower beds north and south of the maze were laid out in Granny Evie's time after the demise of the Great Conservatory. We replaced the tennis courts with a maze in 1962. Dahlias and Michaelmas daisies are planted at this, the north, end. The mop-headed acacias were added to give height here and there.

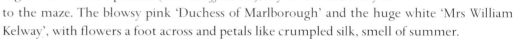

Overleaf Russell hybrid lupins
at the south end of the Great
Conservatory garden in May.

Dennis Fisher, then the Comptroller, designed the pattern which required 1209 English yews (*Taxus baccata*) to complete it. The way to the middle is difficult enough to keep people occupied for a nice long time. There are seats for those who don't want to trudge round – one in memory of my sister, Pamela Jackson, one given by the widow of Fred Carr, gamekeeper, and one given by Dennis Fisher's family. On these you can sit and wait while the squeaks of the lost pinpoint their whereabouts.

When the maze was first planted its paths were grass. It became a mud bath after rain and we got complaints about ruined shoes. But, more important, the trodden paths were an obvious guide to the middle, so we changed it to gravel over hard-core so that the footsteps do not show. The goal in the middle is a weeping pear (*Pyrus salicifolia* 'Pendula'). It stands well above the hedges, visible all the time, and its pale grey leaves contrast well with the dark green yew.

The yews were planted at 18 inches high and soon reached 6 feet 6 inches, where they remain, so the tallest person cannot see over them. Sides and tops are clipped once a year in September. The idea that yew is slow growing is an odd old wives' tale. In good soil young yews can put on a foot a year and nothing makes such a satisfactory hedge, almost as windproof as a wall with the suitable look of a native.

No one regretted the loss of the uneven tennis courts. Just in case someone arrived with a racket we made a new and nearly invisible court below the turbine house, dividing it from the park by a bank of berberis and surrounding it with a high hedge of clipped horse chestnuts. Like Paddy's stone writing table, it has never been used. Once a sprightly American ambassador came for the weekend, bringing all the equipment he needed for a game. To my shame the net wasn't in a fit condition to be used by a representative of the most important country in the world and we could find neither balls nor an opponent, so that was that. But, also like Paddy's table, it may yet come in handy.

Sixteen urns, two on each of the four corners of the Great Conservatory Garden, came from the four turrets of the belvedere at the north end of the house. They are an example of Granny Evie's dislike of Victoriana as well as her reluctance to get rid of anything. She thought they drew attention to the Wyatville wing and so moved them here where they did no harm. When I first knew the family all Wyatville's work was condemned as a monstrous addition to the classical square block of the house. There was much talk of pulling the whole wing down, and if that was thought to be a bit drastic then at least the belvedere and the theatre at the furthest end of it should go. Had it not been for the Second World War of 1939–45, which put a stop to any flights of fancy, it is quite possible that at least some of the building would have gone. I do not know what Granny Evie would have made of the fact that we had the urns copied in 1998 and once again the belvedere turrets are decorated as their architect intended.

In 1990 I saw a human sundial illustrated in a women's magazine and thought we would have one. Here it is at the north end of the lawn. There is a flat stone, 7 feet 8 inches long, with the names of the months cut into it. You stand on the relevant month and your shadow falls on the time of day, which is engraved on bricks at the proper angle. People puzzle over it and no wonder.

Below Dahlia 'Roberta' in the north end of the Great Conservatory Garden.

Opposite The colours in the beds at the north end of the Great Conservatory Garden are all blue-pink with some white. The dahlias include 'Betty Bowen' and 'Hamari Girl' (*above*) and 'Teatime' (*below*).

A hybrid rhododendron in the Ravine. The path was originally made by Granny Evie in the 1930s. In the background is a *Pinus heldreichii* var. *leucodermis*, one of Paxton's planting.

Under Victor and Granny Evie the old, seven-acre kitchen garden, three quarters of a mile away at Barbrook, stumbled on without its glass. During and just after the last war I remember the remnants of those once famous acres being looked after as best he could by Mr Chester. He had been the foreman of a large staff there and when it was finally closed down in 1946 and given to the forestry department as a tree nursery he came to look after our garden at Edensor House. He continued to work there till he retired in 1969 after forty-four years' service. In spite of having a wooden leg which creaked when he walked he insisted on digging 'three spits deep' and piling in manure. He grew good vegetables and soft fruit without equal. His standards were the highest and it must have been a tragedy for him to see his kingdom collapse before his eyes. Yet I never heard him grumble.

After years in the doldrums more men were employed and Granny Evie's love of gardening eventually spurred her on to create something new in the 1930s. She chose the Ravine, the steep banks of a little stream which flows out of the Grotto pond. There she made what must have been a very pretty wild garden in the fashion of that time. She was pleased with her creation and took all and sundry to see it.

A Danish scholar of classical sculpture who came to lunch with her in 1938 described such a tour. *'After coffee I expected to be dismissed and to return to my studies. However, the Duchess addressed me and said "Before lunch you taught me something about our beautiful marble group and I shall look upon it in the future with much greater understanding. Now I will repay you by showing you the park and in particular a flower garden which I laid out myself." The tour and presentation lasted almost two hours. [She was not a lightning guide.] However, it was extremely fascinating to hear the story of every oak tree and the culmination was reached with the garden which the Duchess herself had laid out in an idyllic valley with a bloom of flowers mainly imported from Canada to remind her about the remote years over there.'*

The scholar, Mr Poulsen, then asked the inevitable question, as people do today. *'How many gardeners are necessary to keep the park so beautiful?'* Granny Evie replied, *'We used to have 70 but now we manage with 40. We have to be economical.'*[53]

This sort of woodland terrain reverts to its natural state at speed when left to itself and I am sad I never saw it in its heyday. In 1939, at the outbreak of another war, it was forgotten and nearly all traces of her work were eliminated in no time by Mother Nature. When the area was being opened up in the 1980s signs of Granny Evie were uncovered: a miniature cascade and some small ponds – very pleasing. A number of skunk cabbage or stink lily (*Lysichiton americanus*) have been planted on the stream side and their big yellow 'lords and ladies' spikes come early in the year, before the leaves, which cheers up the dark green valley. As the work of clearing progressed, Granny Evie's stone paths re-appeared in the Ravine, as did some of the old trees. The big oak which appears in the photo of 1935 was still there, though it had fallen. Another tree, a silver birch, now grows out of it. The *Pinus heldreichii* var. *leucodermis* is there, larger than life. One or two *Chamaecyparis lawsoniana* 'Fletcheri' and *Juniperus communis* 'Hibernica' have the air of Granny Evie about them. So do the *Leucojum vernum* which grow by the fallen oak.

A more lasting contribution to the garden at this time was the result of the Devonshires' subscription to one of Frank Kingdon-Ward's[54] Himalayan plant-hunting expeditions. Some fine rhododendrons growing among the rocks above the Grotto are the produce of the seeds brought back – the March-flowering, blood-red *Rhododendron barbatum*, its flower as neat as a pom-pom dahlia and its dark red stem like polished mahogany, is my favourite. Few are named because different species have cross-pollinated. Kingdon-Ward's round-robin sent to the backers of his Himalayan expedition to the north-east frontier of Burma in November 1931 describes arriving at his first camp: *'40 marches from the railhead at Myitkyina, 6000' above sea level ... a queer mixture of plants – six species of rhododendrons grow round the camp. One, a fine tree, is already in bloom. Shrubs of all kinds, crowded with berries, abound.'* The lists of bulbs and seeds sent home by explorers are both long and varied, from *Begonia hymenophylloides* and an unknown *Cypripedium* to species of *Schisandra, Lonicera* and *Viburnum* as yet unnamed. They were received with excitement at their various destinations, but I wonder how much of the hard-won harvest survived. Certainly at Chatsworth the rhododendrons above and below the Grotto are still going strong, but most of the smaller shrubs must have been smothered by coarser undergrowth during the years of wartime neglect.

Granny Evie was very interested in illness. When her tulips at Hardwick got tulip fire she was convinced that she, her gardener and her dog had caught it. What form it took when in the human body I never quite understood. Perhaps it somehow resembled foot and mouth disease, which was another of her recurring maladies.

In spite of these setbacks she was a good gardener and when she moved to Hardwick in widowhood and had more time to devote to it the improvement to the surroundings of that extraordinary house was dramatic. When her daughters and granddaughters married and had gardens of their own she advised them on what and where to plant, and for one Suffolk

Dennis Penrose, the land agent at Hardwick Hall, and his wife photographed in the spring of 1935 in the garden that Granny Evie made in the Ravine. The oak now lies where it fell, a large silver birch growing out of it.

My father-in-law took his copy of 'Bentham & Hooker' wherever he went so he could paint in the wild flowers he found. The entries illustrated on these pages (*right*) come from Holker, now in Cumbria, Hatfield in Hertfordshire, Cales Dale in Derbyshire, Bolton Abbey in Yorkshire, Careysville in County Cork, Ireland and Stobinian in Scotland, just south of Ben Nevis.

dweller she drew a plan which was carried out and pleases its owner to this day. She was a talented painter in watercolours and her paintings reflected her love of flowers, as did her exquisite needlework.

There was another reason for Granny Evie's comparative inactivity at Chatsworth. In 1925 Victor suffered a stroke which, in the cruel manner of strokes, changed his nature. He was not ill enough to give over all his responsibilities to his son, but the nature of his illness made it almost impossible to get decisions on estate matters. Granny Evie could not have initiated any changes in the garden without his agreement and everyone knew that would not be forthcoming. Life must have been difficult enough for her without courting trouble.

Victor and Granny Evie opened the garden for special charities many times each summer. The *Derbyshire Advertiser* of 31 May 1935 drew readers' attention to one such event. *'The gardens at Chatsworth have always been renowned, but in the old days grandeur was their outstanding feature. Since the present Duchess came to Chatsworth she has had great alterations made, and the wonderful rock gardens and the development of the natural ravine and stream on the upper side of the gardens are worth travelling many miles to see. Just now these are at their best. The azaleas, rhododendrons, primulas, and all kinds of flowers border the lovely stream which flows down the dell. The wooded walks are dreams of beauty.*

'The day of the Chatsworth "open garden" is always looked forward to by garden-lovers, so I am reminding them of it in good time. Remember Saturday June 8th.'

Victor died in May 1938 and Granny Evie went to live at her beloved Hardwick Hall.

My father- and mother-in-law, Edward William Spencer and Mary (called Eddie and Moucher by family and friends), had only a short time at Chatsworth. Until Victor's death they lived five miles away at Churchdale Hall, a pleasant Victorian house on a hill above Ashford in the Water. When Eddie inherited the title they delayed the move to Chatsworth while necessary work on heating and kitchen was done in the big house. They could not have moved in straightaway as Eddie was Parliamentary Under Secretary for Dominion

Only three of the eight flowers illustrated on these pages (*left*) were painted in by my father-in-law. He had not found the others. Ronksley is a Derbyshire grouse moor, as is Beeley Moor – both good hunting grounds for high-altitude British plants.

Affairs from 1936 to 1940 and a long tour of Australia and South Africa had been arranged over the early months of 1939. They 'camped' at Chatsworth for Christmas 1938 and moved in during the summer of 1939.

My father-in-law was very knowledgeable about trees, animals, plants and living things of all kinds. He initiated a massive planting programme in the woods to replace hundreds of acres which had been felled during the two world wars. He had made a good garden at Churchdale, adding quirks of his own such as planting electioneering figures, majorities and losses in the West Derbyshire constituency, for which he was MP for many years, in yellow and mauve crocuses. Arriving back after dark on the last train from London he used to go out with a torch to check their progress. He loved daffodils and friendship with Lionel Richardson, the famous Waterford grower, provided him with the newest kinds. In the House of Commons he and some other enthusiasts used to wear the latest bloom in a water-filled glass tube in their buttonholes. My father-in-law described the progress of garden lovers as having five stages. People, he said, begin by liking flowers. They move on to flowering shrubs, then berries. In time they come to prefer leaves and, finally, the underneaths of leaves.

Wild flowers were an enduring interest. I have his copy of 'Bentham & Hooker'[55] in which he carefully painted in a great number of the line drawings illustrating 1,315 natives, also giving the dates and places where he had found the plants. It reads like a diary. I remember him being delighted to go to the north of Scotland for a funeral because for once an inconvenient duty was at the right time of year to give him the chance of finding the *Trientalis europaea rosea*, which he duly did. When he commanded the Derbyshire Yeomanry he made sure the camp was in a different place each year, thus increasing the chance of finding some rarity.

Replying to 'the County' at a dinner of the London Society of Derbyshiremen on 12 November 1949 the Duke announced that Derbyshire had that year added a new plant to

the British flora – *Ledum groenlandicum*. It was identified by Kew. When people asked where it was, the Duke replied that the fewer people were told such secrets the better. As the owner of the land in Yorkshire on which the only known example of the lady's slipper orchid (*Cypripedium calceolus*) grew he was well aware of the risks of people knowing the whereabouts of a rarity.

In 1930 the harvest of one of Clarence Elliott's[56] plant-hunting expeditions to Chile was distributed amongst the subscribers, of whom Eddie was one. He was most generous and gave away a lot of his portion, including bulbs of *Leucocoryne odorata* (glory of the sun) which he asked Mr Weston, the Head Gardener, to send to Lady Spencer at Althorp Park.

The Rose Garden

In 1939 Moucher made her mark by altering what had been known as the French Garden in front of the 1st Duke's Greenhouse. She enclosed it with a yew hedge and planted hybrid tea roses. At that time it was perfectly acceptable for the roses to be grown on their own with no attempt at covering the bare earth between them. We have left her plot as she planned it, replacing both earth and roses when necessary. The roses include 'Felicia', 'Buff Beauty', 'Summer Lady', 'Savoy Hotel', 'Mountbatten', 'Iceberg', 'The Queen Elizabeth', and the newer ones, 'Polar Star' and 'Korresia'; 'Seagull' clambers up the columns. The only addition has been underplanting with pansies followed by mallows, *Lavatera trimestris* 'Silver Cup' and 'Mont Blanc', so that there is something to look at before and after the roses are in flower. Standard gooseberries are planted in front of the greenhouse. As no one expects gooseberries to grow in that way they are not recognised and no one picks them.

The yew hedge was clipped at about 3 feet high. Moucher wanted it to be much higher,

Above Four hundred years at a glance – The Hunting Tower of the 1580s on the escarpment, the 1st Duke's Greenhouse of the 1690s, the clock tower of the Stables of the 1760s, the Rose Garden of 1939 and the Display Greenhouse of 1970 (just behind the 1st Duke's).

but every year she forgot to say she wished to let it grow and was quite upset when coming over from Churchdale she found it had been clipped again. For one who used to arrive on 5 June for the 4th of June celebrations at Eton when her sons were at school there, such a small lapse of memory was as nothing, but she was annoyed with herself every August. (We have let the hedge grow to 6 feet.)

In August 1939 there were three days of non-stop entertainment for the coming of age of Billy Hartington, their elder son. Thousands of people were invited to garden parties and my mother-in-law shook so many hands that on the second day she had to put her right arm in a sling. Brilliant weather held and people remember it as a celebration without equal.

Less than a month later war was declared and Eddie and Moucher returned to Churchdale. Chatsworth housed a girls' school, Penrhos College, until 1946. In September 1944 Billy Hartington was killed in action. The Devonshires never went back to live at Chatsworth. They spent several months of the year at beautiful Compton Place at Eastbourne, which was nearer to London and therefore easier for Eddie to get to his work on the uncertain wartime trains.

In spite of a desperate shortage of labour in the war it was risky to let loose an ignorant amateur to 'work' in the garden. In 1941 a friend of Eddie's, Eddie Marsh, former Private Secretary to Winston Churchill, was run over by a taxi in the blackout in St James's Street and was a bit knocked about. Our Eddie took pity on him and asked him to recuperate at Churchdale. After two weeks he was quite well again and we all thought he would go home. Instead a van arrived with his cellar, including many bottles of his favourite Drambuie. It was then that we knew he had no intention of leaving.

Eddie Marsh had nothing whatever to do so he volunteered to help in the garden. Sometimes he got a lift from Churchdale to Chatsworth, where he did a good deal of damage by haphazard pruning. My father-in-law, who was a kind man and did not want to hurt his feelings by asking him to stop, set him on to moving snowdrops. As he stayed for two years he made quite an impression on the snowdrop population, but he planted them in such unsuitable places that they have had to be moved again. He may have been a good private secretary, but he was worse than useless in the garden.

The girls of Penrhos College were ideal tenants for Chatsworth for the duration of the war, and everyone concerned with house and garden became attached to them and to the staff, headed by the incomparable Miss Smith. The change in garden routine was immediate. The orders to seed suppliers changed from those of flowers, plants and shrubs to those of vegetables. The herbaceous borders turned into onion beds with a lettuce here and there, and potatoes were planted wherever the earth was turned up. All unnecessary work came to a halt. The lawns were not mown and the patches of heather and wild flowers prospered. The Penrhos staff and girls entered into the spirit of the government's 'Dig for Victory' campaign and helped the gardeners who had not been called up in their efforts to produce food for the three hundred term-time inhabitants of the house. In 1940 the Games Mistress, Miss Bennet, helped by the garden staff, marked out eight grass tennis courts on the South Lawn. Miss Bennet herself mowed them with a Ransome 30' automatic, the latest thing in lawn mowers. There was no such luxury as surrounding nets, so the players must have either lost a lot of balls or enslaved younger girls as ball boys.

The Devonshires did a great service to the garden by appointing Bert Link as Head Gardener in 1940. His thirty-four-year stint in the job started unpromisingly to say the least because, when war had been declared most of the able-bodied men had left, except for two or three who were exempted from military service to be occupied in growing vegetables. Bert kept the greenhouse fruit going almost single-handedly and did a brisk trade at selling his peaches, nectarines and grapes (at two shillings. a bunch) to the girls. They saved up their pocket money to buy them as a special treat, having been starved of imported fruit for so long. At the Old Girls' reunions here it is always Mr Link who is remembered. He was greatly loved.

Meanwhile, at Churchdale and Compton Place, in middle age my father-in-law had taken to practical forestry and spent his spare time cutting down trees and sawing them up. He was a fastidious worker and the neatest woodman imaginable. His axe, saws and wedges were kept in the nearest outhouse and every night he disappeared after dinner, dressed in an ancient blue velvet dinner jacket which was impregnated with sawdust, to add to the log pile. In November 1950 the effort proved too much for him and he collapsed and died while at his favourite pastime. He was only fifty-five.

Top The girls of Penrhos College, wartime tenants of the house, skating on the Canal in the hard winter of 1940.

Above The Canal and the South Front in spring. The Emperor Fountain is an ideal wind and weather vane.

'Brought to light'

The early years of the 11th Duke

1950—1970

Portrait of myself by Pietro Annigoni.

Previous pages The Ring Pond and Serpentine Hedge.

Below A view from the South Lawn over the pleached limes to the Cascade House, taken on a stormy day in autumn.

The sudden and unexpected death of my father-in-law Eddie in 1950 precipitated Andrew into the joys and trials of responsibility for the strange place in which we live. It also signalled a full stop in any ambitious plans for the garden. Mr Attlee's government had brought in laws for taxation which far exceeded anything as yet known in this country. Death duty at eighty per cent was levied on all that my father-in-law had possessed. Seventeen years passed before this massive bill, which struck me as a strange reward for a lifetime of public service, was finally paid.

The day after Eddie's funeral Bert Link asked to see me. 'Is there anything you would like us to do?' he asked. I was dumbfounded. I suppose the realisation that Andrew was now in charge and that through him I had a responsible role dawned on me for the first time. After that day Link and I worked happily together for twenty-four years – only for me it was not work but pure pleasure.

Andrew and I, our two children (our third was born in 1957), birds and animals had moved from Ashford in the Water to Edensor House in 1946, when Andrew returned from military service. At Edensor we were within walking distance of Chatsworth and so even before we moved into the house in 1959, we spent a good deal of time there. When friends came to stay it was, as it is now, a source of entertainment – always something to look at, indoors and out, according to taste.

The South Front

The first changes we made, in 1951, were to the South Front. Andrew had the plate glass windows removed and replaced with those you see today. Those in the State Rooms on the second floor have twenty-eight panes each and those in the first-floor rooms have twenty-four panes. The frames, gilded in gold leaf as they had been since the eighteenth century, and sashes were made by the house carpenters using oak from park trees which Granny Evie had had put away to season for the purpose years before. The windows still move up and down at the touch of a little finger.

Although this was not a garden job it made a pleasing and long-overdue change to the appearance of the house from the outside. The Victorian plate glass, welcomed by the Bachelor Duke as a revelation one hundred years earlier, had given that sadly blind look to the building and, as people are drawn towards the Emperor Fountain to look back at the house, these windows are of prime importance to wanderers in the garden.

Another change was indicated to the south of the house. We thought the raised beds on the South Lawn, surrounded with tufa rock and filled with a few thin pink Poulsen roses planted by Granny Evie, were too small for their grand situation. If a flower can be dispiriting it is (or was) the Poulsen rose. The small beds and the miserable scentless plants in them were not fit ornaments for their important place, so they were swept away.

For years I had had in mind a more suitable frame for the house from the Canal and in 1952 we took the plunge and ordered 208, plus a few spare, red-twigged limes, *Tilia platyphyllos* 'Rubra', from Holland to make two double lines running north–south the length of the lawn, leaving 'niches' for the Bachelor Duke's statues. The limes looked small and delicate compared to the massive poles which supported each one. It was the poles that looked like trees and their young protégés like threads bound to them. For years it was difficult to believe the limes would one day be self-supporting and even more difficult to realise that their branches would eventually reach 18 feet 6 inches across – the measurement which we had drawn on the plan as being the right proportion for their important place. A power in the Estate Office, knowing of their exposed situation open to the prevailing west wind, ordained big dollops of concrete to be put in the holes dug for the new trees. The idea was to ensure the stability of the supports – which it did – but at the expense of the roots of the young limes, which could only grow one way. The wires between the poles along which the branches were trained made a pylon effect which we had to live with for years. When the branches knitted together, the supports were no longer needed and all was resolved.

The limes are clipped once a year, in late July. The job takes two men two weeks. They stand on a mobile scaffolding platform and use electric hedge trimmers. The hedge is too

Portrait of Andrew by Theodore Ramos.

Below The sleeping Endymion and his Dog, commissioned by the Bachelor Duke, on the South Lawn.

Above Looking south-west over the South Lawn and the West Garden to the park with New Piece Wood on the horizon.

Left Ivy-covered tufa surrounded the rose beds on the South Lawn between the wars. The statues between them faced away from the Sea Horse Fountain.

Opposite The pleached limes on South Lawn that we planted in 1952 to replace the rose beds. The statues in niches now face the Sea Horse Fountain.

Above The South Terrace steps in early summer. *Verbascum bombyciferum* loves the arid gravel path and sunny position. The bay trees in tubs are taken inside during the winter.

Left The iron window boxes filled with 'Vera Dillon' and trailing 'Madame Crousse' pelargoniums. The pale pink 'Cleopatra' is planted in tubs.

wide to reach the middle by stretching, so the man who clips comes up head and shoulders through the branches, to the surprise of people looking out of the windows of the State Rooms. The appearance of the limes for the coming year depends on the hands and eyes of the operators. They have never failed to trim the long line of trees as sharp as a table top; the acute angles running for 160 yards are a tribute to their skill. When newly shorn, the limes are as satisfying a sight as anything in the garden. In spring the red glow of the twigs intensifies with the promise of things to come.

Another feature of the South Front is the window boxes. I cannot remember seeing such embellishments on any other big country house, but there they are and they must be filled with earth, planted and watered. They are made of iron, of all things, immensely heavy, but as their contents are the only flowers to be seen from the drawing rooms and dining room windows they are a welcome change from stone, grass and trees.

The wallflowers which make a line of green leaves below the first-floor windows from October throughout the winter are called 'Blood Red'. One year we tried orange ones, 'Fire King', but they did not work because they did not show up against the stone, so we returned to the old favourites – ten boxes of forty of them. They make a sheltered place for wagtails to nest and in most springs the protecting plants have to be left round a nest till the young birds hatch and fly. It looks odd unless you know the reason for leaving a tuft of dying wallflowers among the newly planted pelargoniums.

The pelargonium which follows the wallflowers is 'Vera Dillon', a brilliant clash of puce and scarlet, which is a very good do-er. I first saw it in my father's garden at Redesdale in Northumberland and he told me he had it from a local nurseryman who called it after his daughter. Four hundred cuttings are taken in September for the following year. A pale pink ivy-leaf pelargonium, 'Madame Crousse', is planted in front of 'Vera Dillon' along the edges of the window boxes. They cascade down the iron containers and soften the hard lines satisfactorily. How pelargoniums love a hot summer. Their flowers get bigger and better the more sun they have, and are not so good when it is cold and wet. Watering the boxes along the wall of the Chapel has been a worry because there were holes where the iron had rusted away, and the water reached the woodwork of the Chapel walls and the inevitable dry rot followed. All mended now. *Verbascum bombyciferum* (also known as *V. broussa*) seeds itself all over the place on the South Front and would make a silver and yellow forest of the wide gravel paths below the house if left unchecked. This biennial herb has become a feature of this part of the garden, growing 6 or 7 feet tall clothed in thick silver woolly leaves. It springs from a perfect rosette formed from the seed of the previous year. The yellow flowers appear in June wrapped around a cotton-wool stalk that grows at speed. They have a long flowering season. The poorer the ground the happier they seem to be. It is a wonder that they get enough water to survive when growing in the cracks between paving stones. I love them, but others think they look very untidy and are not pleased to see them in such a prominent position. I have heard people say 'Fancy not pulling up those thistles in front of the house.' Some ask for seeds, little knowing they will grow like the plants in the Sleeping Beauty story and overwhelm the rest.

I cannot imagine what possessed the Bachelor Duke to pull down the lovely curved steps of the 1690s on the South Front. The replacements are copied from Chiswick House, London, where they look fine as part of the original design, but here the mass of stone is cumbersome and appears to be clumsily fastened on to the building as well as making the ground-floor rooms dark. Perhaps one day ... He kept the '*two keystones, on which fanciful heads were carved,*

Overleaf The pink rambling Seven Sisters rose, *Rosa multiflora* 'Grevillei' (also known as 'Platyphylla'), on the Elizabethan Balustrade that overlooks the West Garden and the park.

Above The head by Cibber on the South Terrace steps which so resembles my sister Unity.

Overleaf, pages 124–5 The view towards the 6th Duke's bust along the Serpentine Hedge in late April, when the beeches are coming into leaf.

Below The Bachelor Duke by Thomas Campbell. He gazes over the Serpentine Hedge from his Grecian plinth.

probably by Cibber, one of a satyr, and the other as like as if it had been intended for the portrait of Lady Jane Montague, whose early death we lamented in our youth' and incorporated them in the new stairs. The head which reminded him of Lady Jane Montague is exactly like my sister Unity, whose early death I lament.

Below the steps from the drawing rooms to the South Lawn is a '*bronze Endymion worked*', the Duke wrote, '*by Chantrey from a cast made at Rome: it appears to me that the art of casting bronze fit to endure our climate is unknown in England.*' At a Women's Institute festival in the garden in the 1930s my mother-in-law stood by two WI members staring at the naked Endymion. 'Who's that?' one asked her friend. 'Oh, it's Sir Walter Scott,' was the throw-away answer.

Running south from the house parallel to the pleached limes is the '*venerable* [Elizabethan] *balustrade*' which the Bachelor Duke '*brought ... to light from the almost total concealment in which a cut holly hedge enveloped it. The hedge was rather a loss, but it is well replaced by trained Pyracanthus.*' No longer. Now it supports the ultra-fashionable rambling roses which reach over to the yews on the path below. When these rampant climbers first became a necessity in a smart garden in the 1970s (often at the expense of old fruit trees as hosts, which they soon broke with their fast growth and resulting weight) the photographer Derry Moore told me that in every garden he photographed he heard the lady of the house asked 'Is that 'Bobbie James'?' If it wasn't it would be 'Kiftsgate', 'Wedding Day', 'Rambling Rector' or 'Seagull'. A slave to fashion, I have planted all these roses, as well as 'Grevillei'.

The Serpentine Hedge

The next big work was the planting of the Serpentine Hedge in the following year, 1953. I had seen a 'crinkle-crankle' garden wall at Hopton Hall near Wirksworth and wanted to make something like it here. A wall was out of the question, so a hedge seemed to be the answer. At the same time we all thought the bronze head of the Bachelor Duke by Campbell deserved a better approach than the rough path through the wood and one that would draw attention to it. Three big trees had to be cut down to enable the corridor to run its length with no interruption or overhanging branches to stunt the growth of the new beeches, but their sacrifice seemed well worthwhile.

The bust is mounted on '*the column, or pedestal, composed of four circular blocks of marble, which are indeed most interesting, having been part of the Temple of Minerva Sunias: they were brought home by Sir Augustus Clifford; and he had not robbed the shrine, for they had already been rolled down to the sea-beach, where sand and waves would soon have concealed them,*' the Bachelor Duke wrote. In some lights the marble has a sea-green look as if it had only lately come out of the water. He went on, '*The bust was executed by Campbell without any order, and for twenty years, or more, had encumbered his studio; at last I have relieved him of it, and it is to encounter the storms of the Peak in this exposed situation. But certainly no bust ever had so grand a pedestal.*'

It encountered a violent storm in 1962 when it was blown off its grand pedestal and was buried in a mess of boughs and twigs – a sorry sight; but bronze is tough and it survived undamaged. Five forest trees fell across the nine-year-old hedge that night. The squashed young beeches were replaced immediately and a year later you could not imagine the chaos that had been.

Marking out the curving lines for planting the hedge was not easy. We enlisted Dennis Fisher, then Comptroller, to help with this mathematical problem. He and Bert Link pegged it at three or four different widths with deeper or shallower curves more or less defined till everyone was satisfied, and 1,500 beeches were planted and staggered 18 inches apart. The

advantage of beech (and hornbeam, for that matter) is that it keeps its leaves all winter, so the shape of the planting is always noticeable – summer green or winter brown, never naked. The trees were 18 inches high and looked ridiculous in their youth, as if a child had been playing at garden design in a grown-up landscape. You must have faith and patience in gardening and patience is the harder to practise.

The following year, 1954, we planted more beeches to complete the circle surrounding the Ring Pond, and to form an avenue down to the Broad Walk. Till then only half the pond was enclosed and the job needed to be completed. A year or two later a woman read the plaque recording the 1953 planting and I heard her say, 'Fancy bothering to put a notice about a hedge only planted the other day.' The longer I live here the more I realise the importance of doing just that; otherwise everything gets blurred by the mists of time. The mobile scaffolding and the clipping team arrive in August when they have finished the limes, the beeches are clipped at 12 feet on the long sides and 15 feet round the pond.

Set against the original hedge round the Ring Pond are the herms (also known as terms), four-cornered pillars surmounted by busts, designed by William Kent and brought here in 1893 from Chiswick House. I am sure you can find an acquaintance among them – all the faces are people we know, oddly modern in spite of their hair and head dresses.

In the rocks in the middle of the Ring Pond is a fountain which spouts up through the bill of a lead duck, whose claim to fame is that it was made in 1692. In the spring we have to

Above The Ring Pond surrounded by clipped and bound yews and a high beech hedge. The stone herms that stand against it were brought from Chiswick House.

Below Clipping the beech hedge.

Top Eighteenth-century lead urn on the South Front. *Above* Early eighteenth-century French or Flemish marble urn. *Right above* Late seventeenth-century English lead group of Samson slaying the Philistine, in the Rose Garden. *Far right and opposite* Two nineteenth-century marble statues, after the Antique, on the Broad Walk: Venus Pudica and Germanicus. *Opposite far right* Late seventeenth-century English stone bust on the 1st Duke's Greenhouse.

put a plank from the bank into the pond to allow the mallard ducklings to make their way back to terra firma after a swim. (A similar plank is their life saver in the Tulip Pond in the West Garden.)

The herms and the duck are just some of the huge number of man-made ornaments in the garden. Some were made for the place; some have come from other Cavendish properties and have bedded in as if they had always been here so that it is impossible to imagine what it would be like without them: pillars, flights of steps, a Greek altar, lions, dogs, goats, wild boars, snakes, naked grown-ups and babies freezing in the Derbyshire air, a Roman sarcophagus, wrought iron work and pavilions are an integral part of the pleasure of a walk round the garden.

There are also vases, basins and tazzas galore. John Betjeman used to say, 'When you are at Chatsworth try counting the urns.' You would have a job. There are dozens of them of all dates, shapes and sizes, local and foreign, made of stone, lead and marble, tall and thin, short and round, decorated or plain, everywhere you look.

Above A herm by the Ring Pond.
Below The Cavendish snake,
carved in the 1820s, on a statue
pedestal on the North Drive.

Right Inside the Display Greenhouse. The spare table top of Sheldon marble – which is quarried five miles from Chatsworth – supports daturas in pots which come into the house when flowering. A tree fern (*Dicksonia antartica)*, lemons and *Brunsfelsia pauciflora* grow in this Mediterranean climate.

The Display Greenhouse

In the late 1960s we thought the time had come for something new in the garden, a building that would work well and represent some ideas of the latter half of the twentieth century. There was an obvious place for it, north of the 1st Duke's Greenhouse, where there was a real muddle of depressing shrubs and a wretched hut, once the gardeners' mess room. Our ideas crystallised when we saw the newly built greenhouse in the Royal Botanic Gardens, Edinburgh, in 1968. It made an indelible impression on us. It had no interior support, it looked delicate and airy from the outside, and the plants grew well inside. George Pearce was the architect; and in 1970 he built the Display Greenhouse for us at Chatsworth.

Loads of alluvial soil, the legacy of hundreds of years of flooding, were brought from the riverside to fill the beds, and the bricks for the paths came from the old kitchen garden. When it was finished it was like having three big empty rooms waiting to be furnished. These were for growing plants in three different climates: tropical in the 'stove' end, Mediterranean in the middle section and temperate in the east end. It was exciting to see how fast the tropical plants grew; they were such a quick reward – like those which surprised the Bachelor Duke in his Great Conservatory. In three years it was well occupied and the result fulfilled our highest expectations. (But the Display Greenhouse is not universally admired. 'This is the monstrosity I told you about,' I once heard a visitor say to her friend.)

Above The Display Greenhouse. It was built in 1970 and constructed without internal support. Camellias are the feature in March.

Camellias grow in the cool end, and the brilliant yellow *Mahonia lomariifolia*, which brightens dim November days. There are arches of fuchsias, an apricot, and a 'White Heart' eating cherry which would not fruit in the open here. Citrus trees grow in the central, Mediterranean, section: oranges and limes as well as lemons which give off their own clean

Top Hibiscus waimeae.   *Above* Passiflora × violacea.   *Top* Datura 'Grand Marnier'.   *Above* The dwarf banana, *Musa acuminata* 'Cavendishii'.

The seated figure of the Egyptian goddess Sekhmet from Karnak. It is one of a pair bought in London by the 6th Duke in the 1830s. In spite of being made of granite we were advised to bring them indoors, so they deserted the Snake Terrace in 1991.

smell when they come into the kitchen. Ladybirds and wasps are introduced as biological controls of mealybugs and whiteflies. Jim buys these do-gooder insects. Thunbergias climb among them, as do daturas (brugmansia). I only like the white one but the orange creeps in. One of the many governesses who taught my sisters and me used to tell us you go mad if you sleep under a datura. I have never verified this but judging by our education I think she probably had.

One of the stars of the middle section is the night-flowering cactus, *Selenicereus giganteus* (now known as *Carnegiea gigantea*), a close relation of *Selenicereus grandiflorus*, from Jamaica. It never fails to surprise anyone who sees it in flower for the first time. It may be familiar from the illustration by Philip Reinagle in Thornton's *Temple of Flora* in which the clock on a very English church tower stands at midnight and the pale bloom glows in the dark. This *'succulent exhibits to the observer a figure equally grotesque as terrific, with flowers possessing actually the blazing appearance of a torch ... emitting all the while a fine balsamic odour'.*[57] As its name suggests, it flowers only at night. The next morning the cream-coloured flowers, some of which were twelve inches across, hang dead and limp like old gloves. It can produce up to eighty flowers for a single great performance with a few stragglers on the nights before and after. It repeats its June midnight show, but with fewer flowers, perhaps twice more during the summer.

When you arrive in the dark on purpose to see the night-flowering cactus, you must beware you don't catch your shins on the sharp edges of the enormous sheet of grey and white Sheldon marble placed as a low table between the flower beds. This stone, $3\frac{1}{2}$ million years old – thick with fossils of crustaceans from the time when the Peak District was covered in a balmy sea, and still quarried a mile or two from Ashford in the Water – was ordered by the Bachelor Duke as a spare top for the table that is now in the Sculpture Gallery. So like Chatsworth to have two tops for the biggest table you ever saw.

The stove section of the Display Greenhouse is centred round a pond where the *Victoria amazonica* grows at speed (from seed) in the summer. Papyrus and sugar cane also thrive here, as do some epiphyte orchids and the strangely beautiful creeper, the jade vine *(Strongylodon macrobotrys),* with its hanging racemes of flowers like green wisteria. Gardenias produce heady scents. *Jasminum nobile* subsp. *rex* is big but scentless and so is the yellow *Allamanda*. The best tropical smell of all comes from frangipani (*Plumeria rubra*) of Hawaiian garlands fame.

An unusual plant in the tropical section is *Pamianthe peruviana*, which looks like an enormous leek. It produces its sweet-scented, pure white lily flower in the early spring when it makes an excellent partner for hyacinths in the house. It was discovered by Major Pam[73] who gave it to a few friends including my father-in-law, and I believe this beauty is still unobtainable commercially. *Tacca aspera*, even blacker than the 'Queen of Night' tulip, also grows here. It would make a bouquet suitable for Cruella De Vil and some others we know. Next to it grows the snow-white eucharis lily, a relation of the daffodil.

Also in the stove section grow mangoes, paw paw (*Carica papaya*) and the dwarf banana (*Musa acuminata* 'Cavendishii'), all of which produce excellent fruit. Perennial ipomoea (*Ipomoea indica*) of a pure blue, passion flowers – the square-stalked giant granadilla (*Passiflora quadrangularis*) and the brilliant scarlet 'Imperatrice Eugenie' (known now as *Passiflora × belotti*) – climb along high wires, as does the *Stephanotis floribunda.*

The Cavendish plantain or banana (*Musa acuminata* 'Cavendishii') is a plant of historic interest and not only to Chatsworth. Although a native of China, it was growing in Mauritius in 1829 whence two plants were sent to England. One was bought by Paxton for the Bachelor Duke; the other disappeared. Paxton nurtured his plant and, to his delight, it was fruiting profusely within a year. It grew to only 4 feet 6 inches high and so was suitable not only for English hot houses but also for the tropics, where its dwarf habit enabled it to withstand the force of tornadoes. In 1836 Paxton exhibited the banana at the Royal Horticultural Society show in London where the exotic fruit of delicate flavour caused a sensation.

About that time the Duke made the acquaintance of John Williams, the most persuasive and successful missionary who ever sailed the South Seas. Williams spent some days at Chatsworth. *'There was a great charm in the simplicity of his character, his unaffected piety and disinterestedness,'* wrote his host. There had been a disastrous hurricane in the Pacific Islands and when the missionary left Chatsworth he took with him *'many plants that we thought would answer in the regions to which they were bound'.* The consignment included the Cavendish banana, packed in Wardian cases. But later the Duke was to write, *'the fate of poor Williams is well known.'* No doubt his fate was hot news at the time but readers of today may not know that he was killed and eaten by the heathen at Erromanga in the New Hebrides, but not before the banana had been successfully introduced to the Samoan Islands by himself and another missionary, Charles Hardie. It provided food for the hungry people and *Musa acuminata* 'Cavendishii' is now found all over the tropical regions of the southern hemisphere.

The Snake Terrace

Below the west entrance to the Display Greenhouse – and just behind the 1st Duke's Greenhouse – is a terrace, on two levels, of paving stones, brick and pebbles made in the early 1970s. The pavers came from Paxton's Lily House, where they formed the rim of the first *Victoria amazonica* lily pond, and the bricks were kilned at Chatsworth in 1840. The walls that enclose the terrace are built of stone salvaged from the base of the old orchid house, which stood next to the still-existing Vinery. Each slab was sawn in half, thereby doubling the quantity and also revealing afresh the beautiful grain of the local sandstone.

Under this terrace we found pipes with a tale to tell. When beer was part of the wages it was drunk five times a day by all those who worked in the house, from the butler to the fourteen-year-old housemaids. Chatsworth had its own brewery then. The Handbook tells us, *'The beer, brewed above the stables, is conveyed to the cellars by a pipe under ground, 1059 feet long, of three inch bore, the idea of which always gives me a longing, on some great occasion, to form a fountain of that liquid.'* A beer fountain might have been too public for the gardeners, who devised a secret way of getting their own illicit supply. The pipe ran under the corner of the 1st Duke's Greenhouse, a conveniently hidden place from which to tap it. This practice rolled happily on till the strange antics of the gardeners were noticed and the Gardeners' Tap came to an abrupt end.

A star, the Cavendish snake, and stone slabs which once surrounded Paxton's Lily House make up the terraces below the Display Greenhouse.

The lower level, the Snake Terrace, is named after the Cavendish family emblem on its floor, which was drawn by Dennis Fisher and made of pebbles from the beach at Eastbourne.

Above The Laburnum Tunnel in late May. It leads from the Snake Terrace down to the central part of the Conservative Wall. The yews glimpsed on the terrace were left there when the rest of the shrubbery was cut down to make way for the Display Greenhouse.

Dennis was very correct in all his dealings and asked permission from the Mayor to gather a sackful of Eastbourne shingle – surely one of the oddest requests the Mayor can have received in his year of office. The tongue of the snake is made of Duke's Red, the only red 'marble' native to England, worked out long ago from its quarry near by. Andrew inherited a small store of it and Giles Downes, architect in charge of the restoration of Windsor Castle, came here in 1996 and took some to make the cross in the Garter Star which is on the floor of the Octagon Room at Windsor – a bit of Derbyshire in a place of honour. Until 1991, when we brought them into the house, two *c.* 1350 BC granite statues of the Egyptian goddess Sekhmet, from the Temple of Mut at Karnak, sat here, their backs to the wall. They have travelled round the garden since they were bought by the Bachelor Duke in the 1830s, *'sent home by a famous traveller and purchased by me in the New Road'* [now known as the New King's Road]. He put them in the French Garden in front of the 1st Duke's Greenhouse. Granny Evie trundled them along to decorate the Great Conservatory Garden after the demolition of the glasshouse and we hauled them back in 1974 after the Snake Terrace was constructed. Their flit indoors in 1991 was, I hope, their last. Half lion, half woman, these precious heavyweights now dominate the Chapel Passage, where their powerful presence is strongly felt.

Leading north from the Snake Terrace down the steps to the Conservative Wall is a laburnum tunnel planted in 1974 (almost as necessary a decoration as a wild-flower patch if you want to be in the gardening swim). The smell, the bees and the dense yellow are an annual pleasure. The higher terrace, with its pebble star copied from a friend's house, has a view through the opening that we made in the central, pillared section of the 1st Duke's Greenhouse over my mother-in-law's rose garden across the Salisburys to the Serpentine Hedge and the bust of the Bachelor Duke.

Camellias at Chatsworth

The 1st Duke's Greenhouse is given over to camellias. They are a Chatsworth speciality, one of the glories of the garden. One or other of them is in flower from October till May, a flowering season which makes them doubly welcome as they brighten up the dark months. The first to flower is *C. sasanqua* 'Narumigata', a delicate white sweet-smelling single which begins the season in October. It is followed throughout the winter and spring by flowers of every shade from white through all the pinks to claret red. There are a bewildering number, but two stand out: *C. japonica* 'Mathotiana', from an ancient bush which leans dangerously and is supported by a piece of forked wood, and good old *C. reticulata* 'Captain Rawes' which grows in the middle section of the Conservative Wall. The former is the richest, darkest wine-red imaginable, and the latter's wavy rose-red petals with a rush of golden stamens

nearly join together to make a pink glow within the glass.

We have some camellias in tubs which came here after Ronnie Tree[58] left Ditchley Park, in Oxfordshire, in the 1950s. Like everything he and his first wife Nancy had in house and garden, they were the prettiest of their kind, not big flowers but the old japonicas, several of them striped and blotched pink, red and white, including a beauty called 'Lavinia Maggi'.

Camellias will not flower in the open here, but are cosseted in these cold houses and make a great show, culminating in the perfect blooms that are taken to the Camellia Competition at the Royal Horticultural Society Show in London every March. The singles — the deep red *C. japonica* 'Jupiter', white *C.j.* 'Charlotte de Rothschild' and the flecked *C.j.* 'Tricolor' do well. Of the semi-doubles, red *C.j.* 'Bob Hope', and pale pink *C.j.* 'Billie McFarland' are the choice here at Chatsworth. Of the peony-form *C.j.* 'Elegans' usually wins its class, and the rose-form includes one of our own specials, *C.j.* 'Mathotiana', a deep red of perfect shape and seldom beaten. Of the formal doubles the immense white *C.j.* 'Mrs D.W. Davis' can be 8 or 9 inches across. I would love to meet the real Mrs Davis having admired her namesake every spring for years.

Above left We opened the way through the middle of the 1st Duke's Greenhouse in 1970 to make this view. Now you can see across the Salisbury lawns to the bust of the 6th Duke at the end of the Serpentine Hedge without interruption.

Above right Camellia japonica 'Latifolia' and *C.j.* 'Emperor of Russia', and *Eucalyptus globulus* in the 1st Duke's Greenhouse.

Left Ian Webster cutting camellias for the house.

Left Entries for the Royal Horticultural Society's camellia competition, packed in boxes lined with moss and labelled.

Left, below Camellia reticulata hybrid 'Francie L'.

Opposite, top Two boxes of camellias containing *Camellia* 'Grand Slam', *C.* 'Grand Prix', *C.* 'Lily Pons', *C.* 'Billie McFarland', *C.* 'Drama Girl'; *C. japonica* 'Hawaii', *C.* x *williamsii* 'Debbie' and *C.* x *williamsii* 'E. G. Waterhouse'. Other camellias: *top row, from left C.* x *williamsii* 'Water Lily' and *C.* x *williamsii* 'Ballet Queen'; *centre row C japonica* 'Gwenneth Morey', *C.j.* 'Mme Lebois' and *C. japonica* 'Latifolia'; *bottom row C.j.* 'Tricolor' and '*C.j.* 'Alba Plena'.

'Sources of happiness'

Towards the twenty-first century

Previous pages The view from the Kitchen Garden over the roof of Paine's 1760s Stables to the park. The Kitchen Garden was made in the early 1990s in the paddocks formerly used to turn out the carriage horses.

For thirty-five years we paid a good deal of attention to the garden within a few hundred yards of the house. The time then came to go further afield.

Running more or less parallel with the garden wall is the Green Drive, which encompasses all the landmarks we have already looked at. Starting at the West Front door and ending at the Vinery near the top gate out of the garden, it 'serpentises' through woodland and the 'wilder' parts of the garden furthest from the house. Paths lead off it, many of which had become hopelessly overgrown by the early 1980s. In some places the Green Drive itself was just a passage between high walls of evergreens of the most unattractive kind. There was little light, and although the big trees were well above the tangle, their boles were hidden and there were no young trees coming on. Regeneration in the sunless mass of undergrowth was ruled out. Dennis Hopkins was Head Gardener and Jim Link the foreman of the gang who set about clearing many acres of impenetrable laurel, holly and rhododendrons which had been allowed to grow as they liked.

Armed with machetes, like the explorers of old, Jim and his men began their hard labour. It took the winters of 1985, '86 and '87 to get rid of the worst of the self-sown trouble and as we progressed a new world came to light. I have known the garden since 1941 and thought I was familiar with it, but paths, streams and rocks I had never seen appeared out of the 12-feet-high tangle.

The Greek Altar mentioned in the Handbook was one of the most exciting discoveries of this clearing work. It was thought that the altar was long since lost, stolen or strayed. I had often wondered what had happened to it. Little did I know it was under my nose, a few yards from the Green Drive. Smothered in roots, branches and leaves it appeared, none the worse for the experience, on the bank above the Bamboo Walk.

The strength of the growth was shown when, under rhododendron roots, a spade struck lead in the shape of a statue, face-down, which had been pushed off its holy plinth by the branches. It had been decapitated in the fall and the head lay a little way off as in some gruesome murder.

Every day during the 1980s winters of exploration and clearance a new fire was made and the blue smoke, visible from the drive through the park, progressed a few yards. Gradually room was made to plant more trees and shrubs. The temptation to fill all the vacant places was strong, but had to be resisted — otherwise we would find ourselves in the same overcrowded state a few years hence. Though there is no attempt at formality in this 'wild' part of the garden, the voids and masses should be respected, keeping up your interest with changing views, shapes and colours as you walk along your chosen way.

The Green Drive was laid down in gravel over hard-core by the Bachelor Duke towards the end of his reign. Much of it was grassed over later, hence its name, but is now gravel again to make things easier for people in wheelchairs. He also arranged for you to be encouraged on your way by lead notices attached to stones every quarter of a mile telling you how far you have walked. If you are under doctor's orders to walk two miles a day, you could do worse than obey them, accompanying the Bachelor Duke — with long interruptions by me — along the Drive, starting below the Canal.

'*We begin by going down some old steps near the lime-trees; and, having loyally gazed on the oak planted by the Queen in 1832, her mother's chestnut, and her husband's sycamore, we commence this botanical excursion.*' Having followed him down the old steps (or the Summer Stairs) by the limes and gazed loyally at the Royal trees we come to a Spanish chestnut on the ha-ha which was struck by lightning in July 1991. The debris from the flying bark and branches was left as a

Below One of the markers on the Green Drive that tells you how far you have walked.

warning of nature's occasional summer violence. After a few years it just looked untidy, so we cleared it away. Next to the stricken Spanish chestnut is the eighth biggest copper beech in the kingdom. One better than the ninth biggest is all that is to be said about this tree.

At the south end of the Canal is Elisabeth Frink's big bronze *War Horse, 1991*, and Angela Conner's portrait bust in bronze of that artist. These two sculptures divert the eye from unadulterated nature which, however cleverly arranged, can be monotonous. Imagine the garden at Stourhead without its temple or Rousham without its eye-catcher. The importance of such architectural and sculptural artefacts is beyond question and we are fortunate here in having so many. The *War Horse* and the head of Lis are not the end of the story. Other sculptures are already finding a place in the garden.

Angela's portrait of Lis, with its flattened hair reminiscent of her helmeted men, is mounted on a two-hundred-year-old stone gatepost and she looks down the hill to her horse. He is so often ridden that the bronze is shiny under the saddle, as it were. He is hollow like an Easter egg and his eyes have a horseshoe cut into them. Ears back, he has a wicked look, as if he is ready to bite and strike with both fore feet without warning.

A cardboard model stood in his place before he arrived and was immediately christened 'Dobbin' by the gardeners. The big fellow travelled by horsebox (what else?) from the foundry and completed the journey from the Lodge to the end of the Canal in the bucket of our JCB. Lis Frink came to see him installed and I think she was pleased with his place.

She and I became friends through a love of poultry, not art. I have some letters from her in which she worries about the health of a cock called Reggie, and a description of taking

Above The Spanish chestnut tree (*Castanea sativa*) planted in 1816 by Grand Duke Nicholas of Russia who became Czar in 1825.

him to the vet. On 26 March 1992 Lis wrote to me: '*Reggie died the next day — that is to say I kept him going all the week after you lunched here, he began to eat quite well, then I handed him over to a sweet vet near here who specialises in mending birds and small animals. He X-rayed the bird and found he had a badly fractured femur — why he couldn't stand up for long — anyway the long and the short of it — he got him feeding well, took him to his surgery every day, where people admired him! and was sure he could mend the Bone, suddenly one morning he just went. After surviving 2 weeks. I think his old heart just couldn't stand the strain any more. Our builder reckons it was nothing to do with the fight, so does the vet, we think he was probably knocked by a car on the drive, where he used to stand in a daring Monumental fashion. The fight was previous and coincidental — anyway, quelle saga, I was very fond of him. But I have his son who is exactly like him tho' flaming red, black tail, furry ginger feet. He's called RED ADAIR.*' I love the idea of that distinguished sculptress, Companion of Honour, Dame of the British Empire and Royal Academician sitting in the queue in the vet's waiting room with an ailing cock on her lap.

The *War Horse* looks out over the park. The slight inclination of his head points directly to the mill built by James Paine in the 1760s west of the river six and a half furlongs or four-fifths of a mile from the house. The mill is in line with the end of the canal and should, therefore, be visible from the South Front of the house — a significant fact of which I for one was unaware as it is blotted out by trees. I have looked with renewed interest at the horse's outlook. The self-sown alders on both banks of the river will be removed and we will be able to appreciate Brown's carefully planned view as it was intended.

Paine's mill would have been pulled down after the storm of 1962, when two big beeches crashed on to it and smashed the roof, had it not been for Tony Snowdon. It must go, they all said. Tony was staying here and said, 'Don't pull it down, leave it as a ruin.' This we did, to the satisfaction of everyone who sees it — a noble building which makes a focal point by the river for walkers and for people who gaze out of their cars.

Leaving a wrecked building as a ruin has saved many a wonder for posterity. What a tragedy it would have been if the remains of the great abbeys of Fountains, Rievaulx, Bolton and the rest had been levelled. It is like pollarding trees which have started to lose branches – leave the foundations and some walls of a building, or the roots and the trunk of a tree, and you have the basis of what was once the complete picture. Oaks respond very well to this treatment. Several important trees which lost big branches have been subjected to drastic pollarding and are doing famously – one is by the Estate Office, another is opposite the entrance to Edensor village and there are many in the park. It would have been a crime to cut them down.

If you stand between the *War Horse* and the south end of the Canal and look back at the house you see that some genius of the 1690s lowered the South Lawn a few inches so from this point the house appears to rise out of the water.

The big grass-covered hump by the Green Drive here is the ice house. The entrance is down the steep bank. Ice houses used to be important adjuncts to kitchens and dairies in any big establishment. Mrs Tanner, a famously good cook who worked for Granny Evie in the 1920s and '30s, was not satisfied with the ice in it, which came off the Canal. I asked her daughter why. 'Because it was full of swans' dirt.' But they made do very well with it, dirt and all, till refrigerators were invented.

The grass on the steep bank which leads up to Blanche's Vase is slippery in very wet or very dry weather, just as it was in the Bachelor Duke's time. He wrote, '*We pass a brow of the hill, once a great scene of gambols, of sledging, not on snow, but on short turf quite as slippery. The gravel walk below was an effectual check to the rapid progress, which was invested by the sunk fence below with some appearance of danger.*'

The Green Drive winds its way up to the Azalea Dell. Twice a year these shrubs give a memorable performance. On a still day in late May the solid mass of Ghent, the so-called Double Ghent azaleas and *Azalea ponticum* (known now as *Rhododendron luteum*) combine to make a heady smell better than any scent shop and in the autumn the leaves colour well. When you pause level with the azaleas in the dell you can imagine yourself to be in the foothills of some far-away mountainous country. There is a cliff behind you still covered in a solid wall of *Rhododendron ponticum*, and on the opposite side down the Derwent valley looking south is the precipitous tree-covered hill which is Lindop Wood. Not till you turn to the west are you brought back to England with a bump – seeing the needle-sharp spire of Edensor church which appears as if from nowhere.

The ponticum-covered cliff is a tempting place to clear and plant anew, having a sheltered southern aspect. But I hesitate to change a thoroughly Victorian patch, steep enough and big enough to have its own character, even though it is dull for eleven months of the year and quite ugly when in flower.

Bamboos are planted here, there and everywhere. Though they come from the most distant countries on earth, I think bamboos look at home in this garden. They were loved by the Victorians and are part of the nineteenth-century picture when planted near the spiky evergreen trees, tsugas, sequoiadendrons, Lawson cypress and Douglas firs, or with their compatriot cryptomerias as neighbours.

Above War Horse, 1991, by Dame Elisabeth Frink. This was the first important sculpture to be placed in the garden for 150 years. When the sun warms his bronze back children pretend to ride him for photographs.

Below Posthumous portrait bust of Dame Elisabeth Frink by Angela Conner, 1992. Lis looks down on her horse which looks out over the Park.

In 1896 my grandfather[59] wrote *The Bamboo Garden*, the definitive book on bamboos, which he dedicated to Sir Joseph Hooker, the director (and son of the former director Sir William) of the Royal Botanic Gardens, Kew. As a young man in the diplomatic service he was sent to China in 1865 and on to Japan the following year where he spent four years as Attaché to the British legation. The country, the people and the gardens fascinated him and he wrote several books about it, including *Tales of Old Japan*, 1871, an anthology of Japanese literature, describing folk lore and the medieval traditions which appealed to him. At home at Batsford in Gloucestershire he planted an arboretum. He sold the estate in 1919 to Lord Dulverton, head of the Wills family of cigarette fame, since when the arboretum has been added to and beautifully maintained by three succeeding generations.

Although bamboos are pleasing to see here and there, and make a good windbreak once they get going, I cannot imagine wanting to use all the hardy kinds available unless the garden went on ad infinitum. Perhaps my dislike stems from ignorance on my part and if I live long enough I may grow to share my grandfather's enthusiasm for the genus *Arundinaria*.

There are many badgers in this part of the garden. After rain they turn up the grass on the Green Drive with their snouts to get at worms and other fancy food and in the summer they make short work of wasps' nests. In 1997 one took to having a daytime sleep in the West Garden border and as it was big and heavy and a bit of a blunderer Jim Link and Co. were not best pleased, so we shut the door at the bottom of the steps and now he has to sleep the day away elsewhere.

It is extraordinary, when you consider how few people have ever seen a live badger going about its business in the night, that they seem to be the most loved of all British wild creatures. I suppose it is because they have the charm of pigs with a neatly marked black and white coat added. Badgers are welcome to uproot the path, eat the wasps and doss down among the flowers as far as I am concerned. The trouble begins, as with humans, when there are too many of them.

The Green Drive climbs gently eastwards. The daffodils here are those that were forced for the house early in the year; as soon as they finish flowering they are planted out all over the unmown acres. Nothing happens the first year after planting, but when they are acclimatised they behave as daffodils are meant to behave. (Sadly the 'Paper Whites', which smell so sweet in the house from October till Christmas, refuse to flower again.) Luckily no bird or animal will touch them, so they make a good April show and more are added every year. I prefer white ones – 'Mount Hood' is the favourite now – but all, including 'Cheerfulness', go out.

The path twists and turns between high banks where yews and the old-fashioned, scented mahonias grow on both sides. In a clearing a *Sequoiadendron giganteum* was planted in 1998, one of a hundred redwoods given and planted by TROBI (Tree Register of the British Isles – a charity collating and updating a register of notable trees throughout the United Kingdom and Ireland) across the country to mark 100,000 trees measured and entered on their database.

The bank down to the stream in the Ravine is thick with snowdrops. Hoping to make a blue patch for early spring, we planted squills (*Scilla bifolia*) and glory of the snow (*Chionodoxa*) but nearly all have been eaten by pheasants, squirrels and mice, so we have conceded defeat and just enjoy the snowdrops, which for some gastronomic reason are spared by these creatures. The stone paths and much of the original planting of the Ravine was Granny Evie's work of the 1930s which re-emerged as the clearing progressed (see page 105).

Opposite The Azalea Dell, planted by Grannie Evie, in late May. The spire of Edensor church is visible in the distance.

Above Bamboo (*Sinarundinaria nitida*). There are many big clumps of bamboo near the Green Drive, including those on the Bamboo Walk.

The Trough Waterfall

The overflow from the Grotto Pond was piped for some yards down the steep hill beside Granny Evie's old path. This seemed a wasted opportunity and I thought there was a chance to do something better here.

In 1997 we gathered stone drinking troughs which were no longer in use from fields and some from the building yard store, and brought them here to use the piped water to better advantage. This being stone country there are drinking troughs of all shapes and sizes for cattle, one or two in every field which has no stream running through it. As a great number have been superseded by new tanks (though there are still some magnificent stone examples in the park and elsewhere) there was quite a choice for the new scheme.

One by one they arrived by JCB on the side of the Green Drive. Then we had to decide how to place them. They are big and small, rectangular and square, deep and shallow; one is horseshoe-shaped and there is a huge round basin like a cup. There was a good deal of head-scratching about this one. Brian Gilbert and George Morris, the men who know all there is to know about the intricate network of underground drains and waterways throughout the woods, park and garden, swore they had seen a saucer somewhere which must belong to the giant cup. Time went by and it couldn't be found, so we went to work without it. One day it will turn up and I hope Brian will still be there to slip it under the half-a-ton cup.

Each trough had to be slightly tipped for the water to fall over its lower edge into the next one – not too much and not too little. As the biggest weigh nearly a ton this was not as easy a job as it sounds. But Brian is an artist at pointing his JCB in the right direction and lowering a heavy load with precision exactly where it should be at exactly the right angle, onto a foundation prepared for him by Chris Hubbuck and Tony Bird. Sometimes the water falls directly from one trough to the next; sometimes it flows along an upturned stone roof ridge like an miniature aqueduct.

There are thirteen troughs altogether. The waterfall looks at its best in the winter when it is full and bubbling and there is no growth to hide its course. By July it is temporarily invisible till the summer is over and the grass is cut to show it again. In the spring we have to guard the outflow from the pond with chicken wire to stop the ducklings being swept down with the water. The Trough Waterfall is an example of the skill of the Chatsworth gardeners and drainers. No 'designer' was brought here from away to tell us how to do it or to say we were doing it all wrong. Tony Bird drew it in no time and the men who know the place and the materials they are working with have made an excellent job of an idea which was new to them, and have perfectly carried it out. I never cease to wonder at the inventiveness and enthusiasm of the home team.

We seldom call on outsiders for help. Even tree surgery, unless it is extremely hazardous in which case we enlist the specialists, Bob Anderson Tree Surgeons, is done by our men who have been on a training course. Drainers, wallers and the JCB operator are on hand and never fail in these skilled tasks.

Below and opposite The Trough Waterfall. It flows from the Grotto Pond down the Ravine, and is then piped underground to join the River Derwent. Primulas are beginning to seed themselves near the water and king cups are increasing.

The Grotto Pond

Before the Pond itself comes into view you pass between some big cryptomerias (Japanese cedars), ruddy-barked, feathery, delicate and always green. Like so many conifers which are hateful in youth (and worse when in miniature), they are more than acceptable when fully grown. These make a frame for the tree which is a landmark on the other side of the pond — *Pinus peuce*, now over 140 feet high and a champion of its breed. It is beginning to lean and after a windy night I am always afraid to get news of its collapse.

The Pond and its surroundings are a world of their own. The Bachelor Duke describes this as the warmest place in the garden. I have to disagree with that. Nowhere does the ice hang on as long as on this Pond, but if he meant sheltered then he was right. It has the merits of an enclosed place with views and the all-important water. In March the pond heaves with frogspawn and earlier, in a mild January, the witch hazels on the far bank shine like lights.

Below The champion *Pinus peuce* of the British Isles. It was planted at the edge of the Pinetum by Paxton and the 6th Duke.

There are several varieties there, but the pick must be *Hamamelis × intermedia* 'Pallida', a pure lemon yellow. When all else is brown, beige and grey it is an annual joy. The reddish brown *Hamamelis* have no merit in my eyes except that the flowers are curious. There is enough of their colour already in bark and dead leaves so you have to search for them. I prefer them to draw attention to themselves as 'Pallida' does.

One day the swamp cypresses (*Taxodium distichum*), planted a few years ago on the north side of the pond will make their autumn mark — red and brown like the foxtails they are sometimes called. There is one big oak by the Pond. It supports rambler roses; 'Bobbie James' (of course) on one side which mingle with 'Kiftsgate' on the other. The roses have reached high into the top branches and are worth a visit in early July when the tree is encompassed by their creamy white flowers. Later in the year old man's beard takes over and fluffs itself out over the dying rose leaves.

The Grotto is visible across the Pond, but the path turns south of the Pond, towards the Pinetum, before circling back to the other side of the water.

Above left Hamamelis × intermedia 'Pallida'. There is a large planting of this witch hazel on the east bank of the Pond.

Opposite The eighteenth-century Grotto, topped by its nineteenth-century bandstand, seen over the Pond in late September. This secluded place is a haven for insects and waterfowl.

The Pinetum

'This ground', the Bachelor Duke wrote, *'is a new addition from the Park* [eight acres were enclosed and planted in 1829]: *it is much admired, but no two of a party take the same view of it; one extols the scenery, another is in raptures at the old oaks, and a third wonders and asks, why I plant the fir-trees so thin?'* The old oaks are the north-western outliers of Sherwood Forest. Many more are in the Old Park. *'The hemlock spruces are very fine'*, and they are still. *'Near the water there is a grand specimen of Araucaria imbricata, the oldest I have got: it has never had the advantage of soil and compost, that have been found so beneficial to other plants of the same sort.'* The *Araucaria*, the monkey puzzle tree, does not seem to want for anything, being bigger and better than ever.

Alan Mitchell,[60] a man of the trees if ever there was one, came here with Vicki Hallett (later Schilling)[61] in 1993 and they dashed round the garden at speed measuring anything they thought worthy. In 1996 TROBI planted here a *Pinus strobus* in memory of Alan which is thriving to date. I hope it will be worthy of him. *'This is the beginning of the Pinetum, a digression from the order of classing, caused by the fitness of the spot. That is the Douglas pine, the pride of California: in 1829 it came down in Mr Paxton's hat, and in 1845 it is 35 feet high. The green stem and fragrant leaves are its attributes, and it is said to attain the height of two hundred feet, which its progress here makes easy to believe.'* Today, 170 years after it was planted, the pride of California (*Pseudotsuga menziesii*) is healthy enough but it has lost its head more than once in storms, so it has not reached the hoped-for 200 feet. It has a low branch which sticks out at right angles and makes a convenient seat for adventurous children. There is another giant of the same species and date in Stand Wood which measures 12 feet 10 inches in circumference at 5 feet and is 118 feet high. I can understand the excitement caused by these 'new' trees and their rapid growth, so satisfactory to those who introduced them to this country.

Unfortunately we have never found the original planting plan, but must be satisfied with the big trees which are left and plant new as we think best – *Pinus coulteri*, *P. heldreichii* var. *leucodermis* and *P. strobus* among others. I have an affection for Brewer's spruce (*Picea breweriana*) and have planted perhaps too many of them here. I love its drooping, melancholy appearance, and the contrast of the harsh, dark green needles and the soft, pale green ones when the spring growth begins. I believe there is a long avenue of them in some Scottish garden. It must be a strange sight and a wonderfully gloomy approach to a house.

Few people reach this, the farthest point of the garden, and the trees of the Pinetum are probably an acquired taste. But if you like to be alone, to see large specimens of *Pinus ponderosa*, or rarities such as *Chamaecyparis obtusa*, the Hinoki cypress, one of the most revered of the five sacred trees of Japan (it is deemed to have a spiritual presence as well as a practical use for building), as well as a superb view over the ha-ha to the Old Park and the river, New Piece Wood and the next ridge which is Lindop, then it is worth the long walk. You can see the clump of beeches on the highest spot above Pilsley village, near the Farm Shop, from here. Paxton carved his name on one of them, which still stands. Longstone Edge, thought by my children to be 'the Edge of the Known World', is the far skyline. That is the real Peak District of limestone rocks and caves, deep dales and old lead mines three and a half miles distant as the crow flies.

There is a solid mass of bluebells here in the spring. Few photographs portray them as they really are. Bluebells are a feature of the woods in Derbyshire and compensate for the lack of primroses. In the Oxfordshire of my childhood the oak woods were full of both and I miss the primroses so much that we have planted some on the bank below the Canal and elsewhere. I am rather ashamed of pretending that they are wild here, but the pleasure of

Opposite, from top Pinus strobus; western hemlock (*Tsuga heterophylla*); and Brewer's spruce (*Picea breweriana*), a sad-looking, droopy tree which I love.

Above Primroses near the Pinetum. There were very few here till we introduced them in new places. Now they are increasing.

Left Bluebells by the million in the Pinetum at my favourite moment of the year.

seeing and smelling them outweighs any feeling of guilt.

There is a choice of paths before you leave the Pinetum: either continue on the Green Drive or turn right at a big Wellingtonia and walk within sight of the garden wall, the boundary with Stand Wood. Here are some old Kingdon-Ward rhododendrons which seed themselves in the leafy crevices between fallen trees and rocks. We have put a number of seedlings in the nursery to see if any good comes of them.

A *Rhododendron* 'Loderi King George' grows against the standing carcass of a long-dead oak and makes a glorious contrast of young and old when the sweet-smelling flowers come out in May. It never fails. The flowers are

Above Rhododendron 'Loderi King George' whose pink buds open to white.

huge and smell wonderful. Sir Edmund Loder raised it in his famous Leonardslee garden in 1901, a great addition to the bewildering number of rhododendrons in cultivation.

In our garden at Lismore in Ireland they come into flower punctually on 6 May whether it has been cold or warm, wet or dry. As we were at Lismore on that date for many years the smell of this particular flower takes me straight back to Ireland as if I had never been away and as if there had never been another month but May.

Had you not made the diversion to see our old 'King George' you would leave the Pinetum between the Pond and the Grotto itself – another example of the help a building is to the eye in an apparently wild part of the garden. This one looks as if it had always been there and had grown out of the rocks without any human help – pushed into the bank like a wren's nest with the dotty bandstand above. The entrance is framed by rocks which grew stalactites, knocked off long ago by vandals (or Goths perhaps). Many names and messages are written on the inner walls by people whiling away the time on a wet day. It is just as well the door to the Bachelor Duke's addition is kept locked because inside it is not a place to linger. Dank is the word and the barred window high up gives the feeling of a prison: no sooner are you in than you long to be out again. Dr Johnson hit the nail on the head when he said *'a grotto is not often the wish or pleasure of an Englishman, who has more frequent need to solicit than exclude the sun'.*[62] But I am very glad it is there.

The massive rounded rocks like a school of beached whales by the side of the Grotto are a feature which were smothered in the ubiquitous tangle till they were revealed in the 1980s. Some Loderi rhododendrons have now been planted among them. As none of the tender, scented, ones survive in our climate and the Loderis have a hauntingly good smell, they find a place where the ponticum used to be.

Leaving the Pond the Green Drive runs north through the wood, parallel to another path above it near the garden wall. *'Passing on',* wrote the Bachelor Duke, *'you walk over the subterraneous chimney that conveys the smoke of the Conservatory beyond the confines of the pleasure-ground:*

Opposite Rhododendron hybrids originating from a Kingdon-Ward expedition in the 1930s.

Opposite The clearings along the Green Drive are as important as the plantings, complementing each other.

Above Red campion, one of the many wild flowers that grows along the Green Drive.

Top An unnamed maple (*Acer palmatum*), raised from a seed. Its leaves turn deep red in autumn.

Above Sulphur tuft growing on the bark of a fallen oak.

in winter its line can be traced by the absence of snow and frost, but the perpetual spring that I expected to prevail upon it keeps me waiting.' The smoke is no longer conveyed to the tall chimney in the wood above, but the subterranean chimney is still there – a beautifully constructed stone-lined tunnel which has been broken in places so you can see how it is built.

There are beeches and yews here which make good neighbours in spring and autumn, when the contrast between the colours of their leaves is striking. They border Morton's Pond just above you, the least-known place in the garden where you can sit alone by the water on the busiest Bank Holiday. Jim Link planted the *Sequoiadendron giganteum*, grown from seed, in 1955 when he was a boy.

Back on the Green Drive, known here as the Arboretum Walk, there is a giant larch on the right, the one which the Duke said *'was seen by the old housekeeper's father and brought in a pot from Welbeck as a curiosity'*. Soon a long view to the west, cut out of the solid undergrowth in the 1980s, comes into sight. You look down a long flight of steps, across the maze and park to New Piece Wood on the horizon. Edensor church is there and the cleft in the valley above the village runs up to Black Firs Wood on the skyline two miles away. It is a morning view, best seen when the sun at your back lights up the landscape westwards and picks out the ridge and furrow in the park. Jim Link made the steps, a hundred of them, down the bank and cutting through the tall yews bordering the Great Conservatory Garden to show the maze and a big beech beyond it, which just happened to be in line, near Blanche's Vase. The long-lost Greek Altar has been put here to encourage you to stop and look west.

The big monkey puzzle tree was left bang in the middle of the steps, looking a bit mad, like a huge exclamation mark. Andrew heard two old women saying the steps were so steep they must stop half way up, so two seats have been put by the monkey puzzle – a resting place from which you can see into the middle of the maze and its silvery weeping pear.

On either side of the steps we have planted two lines of *Quercus robur* 'Salicifolia Fastigiata', the upright-growing oaks, and my favourite pheasant's eye narcissus (*N. poeticus* var. *recurvus*) which come out very late, long after the rest of their tribe are over, and smell better than any of them. We added hundreds of mauve tulips ('Bleu Aimable') to go with them. Few have survived the pheasants and other creatures to whom tulip bulbs, unfortunately, are caviar.

Above One of the conduits on East Moor, 1,000 feet above sea level, which carries water to the reservoir that supplies the streams and fountains in the garden.

Opposite Glimpses of the Trout Stream as it runs and falls between the Arboretum and the Jack Pond.

Far right, below Giant hogweed and *Iris pseudacorus*. These grow in many of the damp and shady places off the Green Drive.

A 5-feet-tall yellow daisy-like flower, *Telekia speciosa*, and the blue *Campanula latifolia* grow both sides of our walk. They have seeded themselves all over the place since the undergrowth has been cleared away.

A little further along the Arboretum Walk is a child-sized, shallow rill called the Trout Stream which has been brought two and a half miles across the moor from near the Chesterfield road. (There is a clay pit on the moor which is raided when the stream breaks out over the drive and the clay is moulded to the edge to contain it again.) The stream is no more than 2 or 3 feet wide and it has been set on a course so gradual that in several places you could swear it was running uphill. It twists and turns along the side of the Green Drive and then flows through two small ponds called the Spectacles, past the back of the Cascade House, and eventually runs under the Drive to yet another rocky waterfall by the Summer House and thence into the Jack Pond where Angela Conner's water sculpture, *Revelation*, was set up in 1999. Made of brushed stainless steel and resin, this takes the form of an inner sphere with outer 'petals' that open and close, filling and spilling water as the sphere rises and sinks.

We have stopped cutting the grass beside the stream early in the summer to allow some wild flowers to grow and seed. We did not expect the bonus of a great many common spotted orchids (*Dactylorhiza fuchsii*), which have increased dramatically since they were left undisturbed till the end of September. Their early July flowering is a lovely sight: there are so many that they make a pink haze on both sides of the stream. The trouble is the aftermath, dead and dying grass and blackened flowers which look as if no one has bothered

Right The ugly Summer House, *Kalmia latifolia* by its side.

Above The Latin inscription from Virgil and its English translation on the inner walls of the Summer House.

to cut them and take them away. As this is a much-visited part of the garden we put a temporary notice now to explain the reason for the unkempt look.

Behind the Cascade House a yew hedge was planted in 1996 to separate it from the Green Drive above, and to give it a solid green background in years to come. Above is a path, bordered by box, to the Cascade reservoir – worth the climb for the view down the Cascade and across the park to where the newly cut gap through Paddocks Wood must puzzle people who guess it should be true to the Cascade. It is not. It is at a slightly different angle because it is aligned with the pediment on the West Front of the house.

In the Bachelor Duke's time there was a good view from this reservoir of the 'broken aqueduct' which he built in Stand Wood. There are too many trees now to be able to see the aqueduct. You have to walk up there[63] to appreciate its remarkable construction, built of big stones and invisible cement so that it gives the impression of a dry stone wall on a vast scale.

At the north end of the Green Drive is the Summer House – a hideous building of the Bachelor Duke's, which he describes. '*Here is, or ought to be, Luttrell's[64] seat, in the spot he fancied: the style is Saracenic; the columns are of Aberdeen granite, and the rude central capital of serpentino came with me from Palermo, and is the cause of this manner of decoration.*' Paddy Leigh Fermor spotted the inscription from Virgil's *Georgics* and started to translate it. He had not noticed Luttrell's version in English behind him on the opposite wall.

By its side grows an old *Kalmia latifolia*, one of the most attractive of flowering shrubs; its clusters of little pink and white flowers look like a Victorian chintz. Encouraged by this one, a lot more have been planted along the Green Drive. The one to avoid is *Kalmia angustifolia*, a grubby looking red and not a patch on *K. latifolia*.

Near the Summer House is a plot planted in gold and yellow. All the shrubs and small trees here were given by friends and neighbours to Andrew and me to mark our Golden Wedding in 1991. The feathery leaves of the golden acacias rise above the rest and the yellow crab apple *Malus × zumi* 'Golden Hornet' is smothered in bright yellow fruit until the New Year. *Gleditsia triacanthos* 'Sunburst', *Acer shirasawanum* 'Aureum', *Rhododendron* 'Haida Gold', and 'Golden Wedding' are planted here, as well as *Spiraea × japponica* 'Goldflame' and 'Gold Mound'. To complete the crowded plot we have gambled with trying a *Catalpa bignonoides* 'Aurea' in the middle. This patch is a contrast to the rest of the walk, a bright golden-yellow against the dark green rhododendrons which have been deliberately left here to block off the Cascade.

Above the Golden Grove are winter- and early spring-flowering shrubs, mahonias, witch hazels, *Viburnum × bodnantense* and the little *Rhododendron* 'Praecox'. The colour of the flowers of the last is purplish mauve, not very pretty but early. By the time it flowers in February/March it is so good to see any sign of spring that the harsh magenta of the flowers is forgiven. A hard frost and they are gone. Just when the dark days have arrived in November and you think you can go to ground for three months, buds appear on the viburnums and with them, hope. The mahonias follow, their dangling buds ready to come out smelling of vanilla in a mild spell.

On the top path above the Summer House are the beehives. A notice says 'Beware Bees'. I expect we should be had up if someone was stung with no visible warning, but the garden could turn into a forest of notices if you tried to guard against all eventualities. As well as 'Beware Bees' we have got 'Beware Slippery Grass' and I think that is enough to be aware of.

If you dare go past the bees you see some hollies which were planted as soon as the ground was cleared of rhododendrons. *Ilex aquifolium* 'Flavescens' (splashed with yellow), 'Madame Briot' (very prickly with mottled green and yellow-rimmed leaves), 'Bacciflava' (which has yellow berries for a change), 'Silver van Tol' (whose leaves are meant to have silver margins, but they look gold to me), 'Ferox Argentea' (well named the Hedgehog Holly – the leaves are thick with silvery spines) and 'Handsworth New Silver'. In the rare but searching November sun these hollies are shining with health and I am glad they are there, but when you come across a good specimen of the *Ilex aquifolium* species, the common holly, covered in scarlet berries with its association of Christmas in music and poetry, it is worth all the new named varieties put together.

Our hollies are planted in groups big enough to obey Mrs Earle's rules. She stressed the necessity of grouping plants in masses and *'not speckling the kinds about at random'*. Although she was referring to herbaceous borders, that sensible woman's book, *Pot Pourri From A Surrey Garden* of 1897, is full of good advice not only on gardening but also on food and the upbringing of children. In a garden of this size it is even more important to resist speckling plants around.

Among the hollies are several young monkey puzzle trees. A few years ago John Webber, of the family firm of hairdressers in Chesterfield, brought me some seed from a monkey puzzle which dominated the garden of a friend. Its owner said it had never set seed before, but in the autumn of 1986 they showered down and the ground under his tree was covered in fat brown seeds shaped like miniature boomerangs. The seeds were unlike any I had seen before. I took some to a dinner party, where the guests were mostly garden owners, and asked the company if they knew what they were. No one did. Ian Webster planted them and a good number germinated, but it was a slow job. Of these we planted out seventeen among the hollies and several are thriving. I don't know why it is so pleasing to raise trees from seed, but there is an unexplained and deep satisfaction in it and I make the detour to see the progress of the araucaria from Chesterfield every time I come to this part of the garden.

Above One of the golden variegated hollies.

Below The 4th Duke fancied 'strip'd hollies in 10 sorts' supplied by Benjamin Perfect in 1760.

The Kitchen Garden

There were three reasons why I yearned to grow vegetables. Greed was one. Another was for their own intrinsic beauty and the third was to make something out of nearly nothing.

The 2.678 acres of ground which are now the Kitchen Garden were the Paddocks. The reason for the name is obvious – it was the fenced enclosure near the stables where the carriage horses could be turned out. Names die hard here and the older people still call it the Paddocks, though there have not been any horses in the stables for many years.

An 8-feet-high dry stone wall borders the new Kitchen Garden to the east and north, and the western boundary is a lower wall along the track above the stables, which is the 'back door' to the garden leading to the gardeners' car park. The entrance for wanderers from the garden proper is at the south end off the Green Drive. Two dilapidated stone statues of women mark the entrance. They are like real old women, once beautiful, now the worse for wear. They show you the way in.

Till the early 1990s the Paddocks was a dull featureless slope. In wet weather water ran down the hill over unproductive earth. A few rows of vegetables were grown but there was no plan, no pattern and not much enthusiasm. Completing the depressing scene were four Victorian greenhouses, little used and falling to bits. The kind which were common in my

Above The entrance to the Kitchen Garden. The seventeenth-century statues mark the way in. The golden acacias were given to us by the Derbyshire Girl Guides as a Golden Wedding present in 1991.

Opposite The border, which was meant to be vegetables, on the way into the Kitchen Garden. The planting includes Madonna lilies, *Rosa* 'Felicia', blue delphiniums and anchusa, with pinks and pansies lining the path. Fennel, red lettuces and ruby chard for more edible colour are planted in front of cardoons.

Left Lilium 'Casa Blanca' in a tub
and acres of roofs, looking west.

Opposite Vegetables and three of
the four greenhouses that were
spared by mistake.

childhood, with no pretence at prettiness, functional but pleasing to look at, they were built on a high stone platform surrounded by iron railings, out of reach of the grazing horses. Like more important buildings in the garden they have changed places. On the 1897 Ordnance Survey map they ran east –west. On the OS map of 1920 they had been re-built to run north–south. They were built in the reign of Queen Victoria and assumed their present position about ninety years ago.

When the Display Greenhouse and a new glasshouse were being built in 1969–70 Andrew thought that there would be room for everything in them and that these far-away glasshouses would not be worth the considerable expense of making good. He and Bert Link had a talk. The upshot was that he asked for them to be pulled down. Luckily, Link forgot to pull them down and Andrew forgot to go and check. Twenty years later they were put in order, so when a new kitchen garden was mooted they made a good starting point for planning the layout.

During the winters of 1991–2 and 1992–3 the slope gradually took on the shape it is today. Drains were laid and a quantity of old brick – part of a building that was being demolished because of mining subsidence – was brought from Huggeston Farm at Mastin Moor near Chesterfield. The bricks were used to make four raised beds below the greenhouses. The top pair of beds are 36 feet by 40 feet 9 inches and the lower pair are 36 feet by 80 feet 6 inches. They are all about 2 feet high and cover an area of 960 square yards. Huge loads of topsoil were brought to fill them.

Each of these is planted with veg. radiating out from a central apple tree, which is itself surrounded by globe artichokes. The raised beds are edged with the Alpine strawberry 'Alexandra', irresistible to pick and eat as you pass, but a great trouble to gather a basketful for a number of people. As fashion in flowers directs us to grow tired of size for its own sake perhaps fruit will follow and the Alpine strawberries will come into their own. But they will still have to be picked.

We were always going to have a border at the entrance of the Kitchen Garden, but our plan was that the plants in it should be vegetables and herbs as many of them, such as chives and ruby chard, are pretty as well as edible. The duller ones, we thought, could be planted in patterns to make them seem less dull. But it has turned out to be a conventional flower border with a few veg. here and there. It is backed by tall cardoons and some French globe artichokes called 'Gros Vert de Lâon' given to me by Alvilde Lees-Milne. Alvilde had a rare talent for kitchen, clothes and garden and you could be sure that any plant she gave you would be out of the ordinary. So it was with this artichoke – the best of its kind.

Above The famously ugly building of the 1960s and noisy tractors which you might meet anywhere in the garden.

Top Dead and dying trees have no place in a garden and gales destroy indiscriminately. Replanting forest trees is an annual chore. The best of the timber from fallen trees is used by the carpenters.

The hedge of Portugal laurel along the west side of the border hides a building so monstrous that it should be listed and kept as a salutary warning to remind us of the horrors of the 1960s. It was put up in 1969 to house the boilers which heated the Display Greenhouse and the others by the Potting Shed until 1992 (now the boilers are inside the houses) and is constructed of false stone of the kind so well described by someone in the National Trust as "stale cake". It is faced with corrugated iron – not the proper thing which you see rusting gently on lean-tos and roofs of allotment sheds all over the country, but a refined sort which just won't do. Indeed, it is of such horrid appearance that it is worth a special visit but not to be taken in with the rest of the new garden, please.

Close by is the builders' hut which spent 1957 and 1958 by the West Front door, when it was used as a mess room and workshop by the builders who made it possible for us to move into the house in 1959. This hut is now a shelter for machines of all shapes and sizes.

Mechanisation has made it possible for the greatly reduced number of staff to look after such a big acreage, but at a cost of a different kind. The garden is no longer a place for quiet contemplation. The invention and subsequent invasion of machines which do all kinds of jobs once done by people has banished the old calm for ever. When the only noise was a motor mower, that sign of spring and regrowth after the long dead months, it was always welcome. Now rotary mowers, brush cutters, hedge trimmers, hover mowers, strimmers and the whine of the leaf blower are enough to awaken the dead. Add the merciless din up and down the scales made by the chainsaw, which manages to penetrate the deafest ears, and you can forget the idea of a quiet afternoon of reading, writing or just staring in some bosky dell. Tractors and trailers have taken the place of wheelbarrows; and the shredder, which chops up this and that to expedite rotting down on the compost heap, has the terrifying name of the 'Multi Hacksler' and is best avoided when it is working.

We have come a long way since Budding's Lawn Mower was patented in 1830. Sometimes I wish we hadn't.

The kitchen garden is quieter. Its main north–south path takes you past the raised beds on one side and on the other two brick walls containing soil, one rising behind the other like giant steps which run its length. The first wall is waist high, handy for picking the herbs which are grown in blocks for its entire length. Stone troughs have found a practical use on this shelf – one with a tap for water and the rest to grow mints of different kinds. Without the troughs to confine them the roots of the mint would run all over the place. Low-growing, step-over, espaliered apples – 'Cox's Orange Pippin', 'Spartan', 'Laxton's Superb' and 'Lord Lambourne' – are trained along wires by the path above the herbs and Victoria plums give height here. The iron arches over the paths support 'Doyenné du Comice' and 'Conference' pears.

Three iron tubs, like witches' cauldrons, which were used years ago for feeding beans to the deer in the park, were put at the north end of this path. They must be kept filled with earth and planted or they are used by visitors as giant wastepaper baskets. One is stuffed with auricula and the others with whatever comes along.

Above The Kitchen Garden at prime harvest time. The raised beds are bordered by alpine strawberries. Rows of parsley, crops of peas, beans, lettuces and cabbages radiate from the central apple tree.

Left The Kitchen Garden in March when the design of the raised beds can be clearly seen, before growth begins. The straw covers globe artichokes which surround the apple trees.

'Doyenné du Comice' pears growing over an iron arch.

Pears as well as plums are trained on the stone wall that faces south. So many mice lived in this wall that every new leaf was eaten as it appeared and we had to point it with cement. Bay trees grow between the fruit trees. None of us thought they would survive out of doors – the bays in tubs on the South Front are taken in before the first frost and are not allowed out again till the end of May – but now they are outgrowing their space. Admittedly, they haven't had a hard winter yet – so we'll see.

A cage was made for soft fruit. It is not beautiful, but is necessary to keep out pheasants, small birds, rabbits and the devilish grey squirrels. It means that we can grow raspberries, strawberries, gooseberries, black, white and red currants – collectively the reason for staying at home in the summer.

The speed at which all these new schemes settled into their places surprised me – like one of those television programmes when a team arrives to transform someone's garden overnight – and very soon it was difficult to remember what this ground had looked like when it was still an unproductive hillside. Several flights of steps and a grand brick compost shelter finished the job and by 1993 the builders were gone.

There are also conventional beds of brassicas and potatoes, bordered by railway sleepers. The sleepers make a good solid edge. We should have invested in thousands of them in the 1960s when Dr Beeching was busy wrecking the railway system that had been built up with such care (and with help from Paxton). Sleepers must have appreciated in value more than most commodities, judging by their present price. The only disappointing thing about them is they are still apt to weep oil and creosote in hot weather which ruin your clothes if you are rash enough to sit on them. At the north end is an old hut, the Kitchen Garden's private potting shed where an ancient dog sleeps in an armchair of the same vintage while his master works. It has a proper, rusty corrugated iron roof and a little chimney complete with a plume of smoke on a still winter day. By it are no fewer than 82 frames ranging in size from 3 feet 2 inches by 6 feet 5 inches to 3 feet 4 inches by 8 feet 3 inches, which were renovated in 1993.

We have the climate to grow a large variety of the best vegetables in the world in this country and it is disappointing to see them in the shops when too old to eat with pleasure. Brussels sprouts as big as young cabbages, peas as hard as golf balls, enormous turnips which would be fine to feed to the sheep – all these and many more do no favours to themselves or the greengrocer, whereas if they had been harvested a few weeks, or in some cases a few days, earlier they would have been food for the gods.

With this in mind and in the hopes of encouraging people to pick at the moment when the vegetables are at their best I gave a prize for 'a tray of the most palatable vegetables' at our local horticultural show. The judge inevitably chose the biggest specimens, so the object was defeated and that class has long since been eliminated from the prize schedule.

Peas and broad beans are the two best reasons for having your own kitchen garden because it is impossible to buy them at the right age. There is one day in the life of both when they reach perfection – too small the day before and too big the day after. There is nothing sadder than broad beans when they are an inch long and covered in a thick grey vest, only fit for the compost heap. When you remember what they would have been like a few days earlier, you realise with regret that the bus has been well and truly missed. There is no vegetable with a taste so delicate and so redolent of mid-summer as the first broad beans picked when they are even good to eat raw, prized out of their cottonwool pods, easily broken and perfectly tender. We eat them as a dish on their own – not one of the two veg.

with meat – and they never fail to surprise and please. Leave them on the plant for two or three days longer and the grey heaps are pushed to the side of the plate, a waste of time to grow, pick and cook. 'The Sutton', 'Hylon', 'Witkim Manita' and 'Masterpiece Green Longpod' are the ones we grow.

It is the same with peas. Not only must they be picked and eaten on the same day, but it must be THE day of perfection. The poetic descriptions of the qualities of the endless varieties listed in the catalogues make you long for them all. Don't be taken in. As with nearly every kind of vegetable there are only one or two worth growing and I look forward to the day when a seed merchant admits this and states after some thrilling name 'Not worth growing, too tough and impossible to cook, stringy, tasteless, apt to rot in the ground ...'. So many suppliers have caught the dishonesty of politicians and pretend everything in the garden will be rosy as long as you buy their wares.

The list of peas is so long and muddling that you are left wondering which to plant and repeating the names: 'Onward', 'Lord Chancellor', 'Daybreak', 'Feltham First' and the three Kelvedons – 'Monarch', 'Triumph' and 'Wonder'. Forget them all, except the peerless 'Hurst Green Shaft' – the only pea to grow. Plant it every two weeks throughout the spring and eat it on the right day on its own, like broad beans. Only then will you know what green peas ought to taste like.

Runner beans are a different matter and better grown as something to look at rather than to eat. Again the catalogues list pages of them, some of the names – 'Enorma', 'Goliath', 'Prizetaker' – being a giveaway of the big, tough, inedible, foot-long things that they will become. Grow them, if you must, as creepers round the front door or mixed with the apples on the arches over the garden path where their orange flowers look quite pretty.

If you have got room, an unusual vegetable which, I think, is well worth growing is the squash. However, it is not suitable for a small garden because it suddenly takes off and snakes over a lot of ground. Like peas and beans, squash must be eaten at the right size and not allowed to get much bigger than a tennis ball. 'Little Gem', not to be confused with the lettuce of that name, is one we grow. The other, whose inside is like spaghetti when cooked and has to be explained to guests who look questioningly at it, is called, curiously enough, 'Spaghetti'. I think it is good.

Celery is trickier. The best bit to eat is the root, so the great thing is not to allow it to be cut off and thrown away. You have to be very quick about this or it will be gone. It is impossible to buy it with the root on so the only hope is to grow it. The pests and diseases to which all celery is prone are legion. The possible (no, probable) catastrophes of the celery world are minerfly, cutworm, boron deficiency, cucumber mosaic rot, damping off and sclerotinia rot. Their hearts can be rotten or even missing, and then there are snails and slugs, and soil too wet or too dry to suit these fussy hypochondriacs. If you can keep such disasters at bay and get a good root to eat with Lord Chewton's Cheddar cheese you have got perfection.

Sea kale, asparagus and Jerusalem artichokes are luxuries which have come with the Kitchen Garden. The edible sea kale, *Crambe maritima*, is a relation of the fashionable *Crambe cordifolia* so often seen in borders. Sea kale tastes different from anything else and people often ask what it is. In November earth is heaped up over the plants and big wooden boxes with thick handles on the lids are put over the mounds. The blanched leaves and stalks grown in the dark appear in the early spring when fresh vegetables are scarce. When you have eaten enough and its season ends, the boxes are removed and it can grow as it pleases

Courgettes in flower. Like most vegetables, they are best eaten when they are small and young – in their case, soon after the flowers fade.

Opposite Leeks and celery for
winter eating.

Top left Tiger lettuce and endive.   *Above* Rhubarb, or ruby, chard.   *Top right* Mange-tout peas.   *Above* 'Masterline' and 'Red Sprout
Rubine' Brussels sprouts
in early summer.

Tim Walton picking 'Lollo Rosso' lettuces which are very pretty but tasteless. The box surrounds marjoram grown in a stone trough. Globe artichokes can be seen in the background.

and gather strength for next winter through its pretty blue-green leaves.

Jerusalem artichokes are the ingredient for the second most delicious soup. My first prize goes to sorrel, but the artichoke version runs it close — it is the essence of autumn. They grow very tall and end up like young trees.

After sea kale, another early spring treat is purple sprouting broccoli which comes thick and fast in a mild February. If it is spared by the pheasants and if you can make it last until the asparagus begins you have the best of all worlds.

Asparagus must be the greatest luxury of the vegetable kingdom, partly because it is delicious to eat and its short season leaves you longing for more and partly because it comes in the best weeks of the year. (God preserve me from imported asparagus available all the year round. It is a travesty of the real thing.) Until the new Kitchen Garden was made we never had enough and it was strictly rationed. Shades of my sister Pam, a great grower and cook of vegetables from her Cotswold garden: 'How are you?' I telephoned to ask her one May. 'Oh, living on the fat of the land – just enough asparagus for one'. Here it might have stretched to two, but no more. Now things are looking up.

Leeks — have you seen them at a northern produce show? Or even in the soft underbelly of the south at the Royal Horticultural Society's Fruit Show held in October in London? They are a revelation — so big, long, fat and clean that they are hardly recognisable as leeks, they are exciting, strange and beautiful green and white pillars with roots like a mane of hair several feet long. What they taste like I do not know. Ours are more normal and taste perfectly all right as the essential ingredient of winter dishes. They are another matter when small and thin, cooked whole and tackled on the plate with a fork. It's the same old story: if you have to use a knife to battle through a stringy bit they are too old.

At shows you find onions as big as your shiny bald head with neatly tied and folded ends of leaves at the top. *The Vegetable Finder* lists 144 named varieties, so Heaven knows how you choose which one to grow. I think it is better to buy them from the fellow in a beret who hangs them over the handlebars of his bicycle so that we can get back to peas and beans.

Of lettuces, cos are the ones to go for, but oh what a trouble they are to look after. They must be tied with raffia, never a leaf out of place, not just once but as they grow. So unless you have time on your hands you had better forget this crisp, dark green and white delicacy and stick to 'Little Gem', a semi-cos which is the most reliable of its kind; much better than the floppy, dark red 'Lollo Rosso', which looks all right but tastes nothing like as good. 'Little Gem' has a heart so crisp that if you are lucky enough to land it out of the salad bowl onto your plate, it is like getting the sixpence in the Christmas pudding. To the dismay of your neighbour you sound like a goat eating a cabbage stalk when you start to chew it. 'Tom Thumb' is the next best thing.

A linguistic puzzle of the vegetable world is chicory and endive. They are the opposite in French and English and I never can remember which is which, so instead of the delicious fat, white torpedo-shaped winter object, which is equally good raw in salad or cooked with meat, I find a crimpy green leaf which looks quite pretty but is tasteless. The kitchen part of the Kitchen Garden is fraught with difficulty.

We grow three varieties of chicory – 'Brussels Witloof', 'Rossa di Verona' (radicchio) and 'Sugar Loaf'. The first two are sown in the open in May. 'Brussels Witloof' needs a certain amount of fussing over – it must be lifted in October and stored in damp sand, then brought into the greenhouse as required, put in boxes under the staging, watered and kept in the dark for 2–3 weeks until white and crisp and ready to eat. 'Sugar Loaf' is sown outside in June, lifted in October and stored in boxes with the roots in damp compost. The outside leaves decay and look horrible, but the inside makes the best of salads.

Sorrel is the sharpest, freshest and most rarely met-with of the leaf vegetables. Ours came through my sister Pam, the queen of veg. (I thought her epitaph ought to have been 'And May Spinach Perpetual Shine Upon Her', but it was over-ruled.) She got it from Robin Adair, an excellent cook who was a great friend of X. Marcel Boulestin, the *patron* of the best restaurant in London in the 1930s. So it has come down to us through the famous, and its own claim to fame is that it does not bolt and run to seed like other sorrels but puts its energy into spreading. The leaves from one root will turn a spring soup into nectar and it will keep on growing and giving itself up to the kitchen with no trouble at all.

People have suddenly twigged that there are potatoes other than the maincrop varieties which are so easily bought it is hardly worth bothering to grow them. 'Pink Fir Apple' is available from supermarkets at last but we grow it all the same. 'Ratte' too, and 'Wilja', 'Foremost' and 'Noisette', as well as the good old 'Duke of York'. I feel sorry for people who are on a diet which forbids potatoes. They are one of the great pleasures of life.

Other root vegetables which cheer the kitchen are autumn-sown turnips, whose leaves can be cut several times in March and April and cooked like spinach. We sow 'Purple Top Milan' and 'Tokyo Cross' in spring for harvesting in late summer and again in autumn for over-wintering.

The produce of the Kitchen Garden is a joy matched only by the names of some vegetables, which stretch the imagination. The romantic 'Tender and True' is, believe it or not, a parsnip. There is a pea called 'Bikini' and the best-known radish is 'French Breakfast'. I have never met a Frenchman who demands radishes for breakfast but he must exist. How did 'Pink Fir Apple' turn into a potato or 'Whinham's Industry' a gooseberry? What are 'Butcher's Disease Resisting', 'Balder', 'North Holland Blood Red', 'Mammoth Sandwich Island' and 'Early White Stone'? They are A-level exam questions for the vegetable grower.

The greenhouses which should have been pulled down are used to grow melons, tomatoes, cucumbers, the 'Vera Dillon' pelargoniums for the window boxes, pot plants to sell, herbs in the winter, and forced potatoes, chicory (or is it endive?) and rhubarb. The week of the New Year brings the pale pink forced rhubarb, which is fresh, new and welcome after rich Christmas food.

The lean-to where some orchids are grown is a secret place because I never have the right key for the impossible padlock. I am told that my favourite chalk-white coelogyne grows there and twenty other kinds, but as I cannot get in I am unable to verify this.

Melons in the Victorian greenhouses. Those on the bench are 'Sweetheart'; those hanging are 'Emerald Gem'. Each has its special taste and consistency lost, alas, on me, as I don't like them. But the chickens adore the seeds.

Left Annuals, including *Cosmos bipinnatus* 'Picotee', *C.b* 'Purity' and *Convolvulus tricolor* Ensign Series, crowded together in a border in August.

Jim grows flowers for cutting in the Kitchen Garden. Delphiniums of all the blues, dahlias of shocking proportions, asters both double and single, sweet peas, the tall, double antirrhinum 'Madame Butterfly', mixed-colour helichrysums — everlasting flowers from yellow to bronze which are nature's dried flowers and are immensely popular with our visitors, cleome and horrible stachys. Of the spray chrysanthemums, I always hope for yellow, pink and white but bronze turns up like a bad penny. Lupins for the Great Conservatory Garden start life here too.

A block of tulips for picking is planted above the border. All the Viridiflora Group, some fantastic Parrots, and 'Queen of Night', as nearly black as a flower can be, are its stars. The trouble is I can hardly bear to pick them as they look so fine growing altogether.

There are annuals too, in all colours of the rainbow. We make no attempt to plan; the seeds are piled in and left to make the kaleidoscope of colour and shapes which is an eye-catcher in July and August. There is no careful good taste; the oranges, mauves, blues, pinks, reds and yellows take their chance and clamber over one another, the strong smothering the weak. It really does look like the illustrations in a seed catalogue which enliven January evenings when you sit by the fire trying to imagine what will happen six months hence. It is the very opposite of the White Garden at Sissinghurst. We have never had a white garden, which may be an inherited prejudice. My mother did not like white flowers — she used to say they were like bits of paper blowing about.

In 1998 a stream was conjured up of water which was previously piped underground, the idea being to make a pond in which we could grow watercress. The plan was drawn up in one evening by Tony Bird and constructed by that incomparable pair of wallers, David

Opposite Sweet peas climbing over a wigwam above all the annuals you can think of, muddled up close together for a dazzling result.

Spencer and Ian Fletcher. In a few months the pond was lined with stone and the water came out of its pipe, looking and sounding as we hoped. Part of the stream runs over sharp riven gritstone, from nearby Freebirch Quarry, set close together and upright, a pale copy of one which I had seen in the garden at the new Getty Museum in Los Angeles. David Spencer made a waterfall which tumbles down the stone platform below the greenhouses and lands between two beds of lavender contained by golden box. The water, the mauve and the yellow are a good combination.

Watercress was planted. Some came from the gin-clear stream which runs through the limestone cleft made by the River Wye just off the A6 below Monsal Dale. To back it up Jim bought some from an unlikely source, our Farm Shop, and Ian rooted them. We all thought the ever-flowing pure spring water coming out of the hill would be just what the watercress needed to grow on the gravel bed prepared for it. What we had not reckoned with were the mallard ducks. They soon ate what we were hoping to eat, so it is another of what the Duke of Windsor used to call his 'horticultural disappointments'.

The Kitchen Garden is, like all gardens, a source of endless pleasure and some frustration but the pleasure outweighs the frustration a thousand-fold.

Below the beech hedge at the bottom of the Kitchen Garden there is a little apple orchard. Here is the obligatory wild-flower patch on a pretend cornfield. The old enemies of the arable farmer – cornflowers, corncockles, corn marigolds, poppies and the fascinating little multi-coloured heartsease pansies – are now the fashion. People should be warned that wild flowers need as much nannying as an Edwardian border and it is no wonder they are disappointed when nothing happens after throwing a packet of seeds onto the ground and expecting it to look like Highgrove.

In spite of ploughing and as-it-were harrowing (raking – no room for a proper harrow here), and generally giving it the treatment that cornfields get but minus the sprays, this patch seldom turns out right. For one thing the oats, barley and wheat, which, after all, are the point of a cornfield, seldom germinate as they are scratched up and eaten by the birds of the air as soon as they are planted. And one or other of the loved weeds does better than the rest, so you never get the ideal mixture of blue, yellow and red. Never mind, we must persevere with our cornfield wild-flower patch. On the left of the path is the so-called hayfield. Buttercups are apt to take this over. They are very pretty, but would make unpalatable hay for any cow unlucky enough to be offered it. Cows are too clever to eat it, knowing instinctively that buttercups are poisonous. Ragged Robin, white and pink campion, yarrow, knapweed, ox-eye daisy, several kinds of thistle and, I must admit, some decent clovers do look nice and remind me of the fields round Swinbrook when I was a child during the agricultural depression of the 1930s.

Left, from top The Kitchen Garden stream. Made in 1998, the stream runs over sections of flat and of riven stones (and also widens to make a pond for watercress), and then splashes down a waterfall. Primulas grow by its side at the top and vegetables and herbs by the lower section. The water is then piped underground till it reappears at the top of the stone bastion which supports the greenhouses to make another waterfall.

Right Corn marigolds and cornflowers are among the wild flowers in the little apple orchard below the Kitchen Garden.

The Cottage Garden

At the Chelsea Flower Show in 1988 there was an outstanding exhibit called 'A Country Woman's Cottage Garden' put on by Cheshire Women's Institutes with help from Bridgemere Nurseries. We thought a garden on that scale would be a welcome change here.

At about the same time I saw something which appealed to me greatly in the wonderful Dorset garden made by my sister-in-law and her husband, Anne and Michael Tree. Anne is an original with perfect taste and an inventor, not a follower of others. She had got a blacksmith to make the iron framework for the base, back and posts of a four-poster bed, a bedside table and a roomy armchair. Box was then planted and trained to follow the shape of the iron bed and vines were grown up the bedposts so that grapes hung down from its tester. The bedside table was formed of variegated ivy over an iron table and a rambler rose covered the armchair, easily mistakable for a Colefax chintz when in flower but probably not so comfortable to sit on.

While the WI garden became the starting point for our own Cottage Garden, plus the inevitable vegetable patch and chicken run, Anne's invention led us to think of the 'cottage' itself, and the result is there for all to see.

The 'cottage' sits on two levels. We built a stout wall against the back of the ground floor and planted a yew 'staircase' to lead to the bedroom above. Downstairs are two upright chairs and a dining table of privet, the latter covered with a cloth of red and white begonias, and a golden privet sofa, fire surround and mantelpiece. The fire is artemisia – for grey ashes, and red pelargoniums – for the flame. Upstairs is a four-poster bed draped in the large-leaved ivy *Hedera canariensis* 'Ravensholt'. The bedspread, planted to look like chintz, is changed each year and the pillows are begonias in squares. At the foot of the bed is a forsythia chaise-longue and the lamps on the bedside tables have 'Tiffany' shades of ivy grown over children's umbrellas. The dressing table is privet with an ivy looking-glass, and the carpet is thyme.

The front garden has beds bordered by box, filled with Parrot tulips and forget-me-nots in spring followed, in autumn, by 'Coltness Gem' dahlias, the delight of butterflies and bees.

Its own little vegetable patch is only 42 × 28 feet, but is useful in that it shows what a lot of food can be grown in a small space. It produces all sorts, from rhubarb and strawberries to peas, beans and herbs. The oak fence which surrounds it is not sawn but riven with an axe. Jim Link and Peter Tanner made it from a fallen tree. Jim told me how it was done. 'You must have a straight grain piece of oak with no knots. It is split by using wedges and an axe. Place the wedge at one end, tap with a hammer until it bites into the wood and a small split appears. Put a second wedge behind the first to encourage the split to follow the grain down the wood. Continue this processs until the length is split in two. Carry on splitting till the wood is the required width, then shape with a sharp axe.' This reads like a cooking receipt, but it is not quite as easy as boiling an egg and perhaps should not be tried by those who are not in daily contact with hammers, wedges and axes. The result is like the fencing in eighteenth- and nineteenth-century paintings of farmstock and in some of Stubbs' paintings of racehorses. Though never seen now, it strikes a chord in the memory of anyone who has looked at those very English pictures. The wood has not been treated in any way and so has become the silvery-grey colour of oak exposed to the weather. Old men lean on the fence discussing veg. and sometimes I hear them say how much better theirs are.

People arrive at the Cottage Garden and stare for a while, wondering what on earth they are looking at. Then they start laughing and getting out their cameras. If they think it is too whimsical for words they can walk by and go on to the big Kitchen Garden.

Above Parrot tulips and forget-me-nots in the front garden of the Cottage Garden in May.

Opposite above The box enclosures of the front garden.

Opposite below The vegetable plot behind the Cottage Garden.

Overleaf The Cottage Garden in September. The 'furniture' is fully clothed, and 'Coltness Gem' dahlias fill the box-edged beds. The 'tablecloth' is begonias.

Below Allium 'Globemaster' in the vegetable plot.

Above Harvested onions hanging on the shed wall in the Kitchen Garden.

Overleaf pages 182–3
Main picture 'Muscat of Alexandria' grapes, a speciality at Chatsworth. The leaves begin to turn in October.
Top right The Muscat vines in early spring, when the stems are scraped to eradicate any red spiders or mealybugs.
Bottom right 'Madresfield Court' black grapes.

Below the Cottage Garden is the Potting Shed, that birthplace of horticultural skill.

The smell inside is one of the few that is unchanged since my childhood. Breathe in and I am transported seventy years back in time to the Swinbrook equivalent. It smells sometimes of damp earth and tarred string, sometimes of apples, sometimes of scented flowers picked and plunged in a bucket or sometimes – a glorious moment – of the first forced hyacinths at Christmas.

When we lived at Edensor in the early years of our marriage, an important part of the decoration of the potting shed there was Mr Chester's straw hat. It spent the winter on its hook above a cascade of raffia. When he decided the sun was strong enough in April, or in a cold spring delayed till May, he took it down, gave it a quick dusting and wore it till September. Never mind the calendar, the day his straw hat came out was the real first day of spring.

At Chatsworth there is an inner room in the Potting Shed, the office where Barbara Burchby makes out the orders, checks bills, does the accounts, and sees to the wages, the deliveries and the takings from the summer sales of flowers and vegetables. She takes orders for wedding bouquets, wreaths for Christmas and funerals; lists the evergreens which decorate the Cavendish Hall in Edensor for functions, the church flowers and the posies for the tables at the Carriage House Restaurant; and sends flowers to Ashgate Hospice every fortnight. In consultation with Jim, Barbara also does the budgets in December for the following year. These budgets are high on the list of garden pests and put a stop to all sorts of schemes which, were it left to woman's intuition, would be so happily carried out. Having wrestled with all the above, a different and more pleasant duty of Barbara's is watering the plants in the house.

Having visited the Potting Shed and seen all that goes on there you will find the names of our dogs of yesteryear carved into a stone gatepost near by. I think a big garden needs something alive and moving so Buff Cochins are at large here. Their feathered legs discourage them from too much scratching and they stand and walk in stately fashion, never straying far from their house and their shrubbery where they retire for safe haven from toddlers and visiting dogs. They must be the most photographed poultry in the land and Jim must be the only head gardener to put up with chickens on the loose.

Near the Potting Shed are two glasshouses. One is the new Commercial House (there is not much commerce about it but never mind); the other is the Vinery. The white 'Muscat of Alexandria' grapes inside were planted in 1921, replacing orchids. They are grown in a curious way which I have never seen elsewhere. There is a contained central 'bed' which runs down the middle of the house. The fibrous stems of the vine reach the pitch of the 16-feet-high glass roof and fruiting branches are tied on horizontal wires making a canopy when in leaf and so that the grapes hang from above. In August, before any have been cut, there is no prettier or more tempting sight than bunch after bunch of the almost translucent golden-green fruit repeated again and again to the end of the house.

The Muscats have a long season, starting in mid-August and going on till the New Year, by which time they have started to shrivel and are on the way to becoming raisins. There is

nothing haphazard about their upbringing. Their year begins, suitably, in January, when they are pruned. Two inches of fresh loam replaces the existing top soil. This loam is the result of cutting and stacking turf twelve months earlier. The turf stack looks like a gingerbread house in a fairy story. It is broken up and brought into the Potting Shed in August, shredded and used as above.

In February the stems of the vines are scraped to remove loose bark and unloved insects and to make it easier for the 'eyes' to break in spring. They are fed with dried blood and bonemeal. In March the ventilators are closed and during one week some heat is gradually introduced. The vine 'rods' are sprayed with tepid water to help the buds break and grow. The buds are 'stopped' at two inches long and the laterals are tied to the wire and iron supports. In May they flower and are rewarded with another feed. When the grapes are the size of a pea they are thinned with scissors: a third to a half are removed so that the rest can swell. Thinning continues throughout the summer and they are fed every six weeks till the grapes are ripe. Then the bed is covered with dry straw to hold moisture, because they are not watered again till January.

Looking at the luscious results of this highly skilled and laborious work, my daughter Sophy, then aged seven, said ,'You know, Mum, the wonderful thing about these grapes is that they're free.'

Peaches and nectarines are grown in the north end of the Vinery and in the Conservative Wall. Of the peaches, 'Peregrine', 'Rochester', 'Hale's Early' and 'Dymond' follow one another in glorious succession. The nectarines 'Early Rivers', 'Lord Napier' and 'Pineapple' run them close. A nectarine called 'Pineapple' is enough to muddle anyone and reminds me of one spring at Lismore when someone brought Cyril Connolly to stay. He fancied he knew something about plants and, looking at the flowers of a pink and white chaenomeles (then generally known as japonica) said to my daughter Emma, who does know something about plants, 'Which japonica is that?'. To which she replied, correctly, 'Apple Blossom'. 'Oh no it isn't,' said Cyril, 'It's a japonica.' Emma made a pitying face and did not pursue the matter.

Above Buff Cochin cock and hens at large near the Potting Shed.

Below The finest 'Royal George' peach in the country was grown at Chatsworth by the 6th Duke. Illustration from *Pomona Londinensis* by William Hooker, 1818.

181

Epilogue

Andrew and I are ever conscious of how lucky we are to live in such a beautiful place and to work with people who have the welfare of Chatsworth at heart. Without the gardeners there would be no garden. In our time Bert Link, Dennis Hopkins and Jim Link in turn have led a team of men and women who have made it what it is today, keeping up the tradition of excellence, while tending these acres of natural and man-made beauty and ensuring that our visitors are made welcome.

The gardening profession seems to provide a settled existence which induces a habit of long service. At beautiful Levens Hall in Cumbria there have been only ten head gardeners since 1710, an average of 30.6 years each – surely a record which will never be equalled. At Chatsworth seventeen gardeners have received a special present for having completed forty years' work since 1963 and eight others have done twenty-five years or more.

The last three heads have led the way, each having completed fifty years work here. Bert Link came from Kent in 1924 and was head from 1940 till his retirement in 1974. When Andrew was a little boy it was Bert who chased him out of the peach houses. They remained life-long friends. Bert was followed by Dennis Hopkins and both men started their careers washing flower pots. Dennis came in 1939 and was greenhouse foreman for thirty-nine years till he took over from Bert. There is little Dennis does not know of the skills of the stove. Jim Link, Bert's son, succeeded Dennis as head in 1989. He had worked in the Forestry team from 1950 and trees are still his first love. I do not know if these records of long service are unique, but I do know that Chatsworth owes a huge debt to Bert, Dennis and Jim. Their half-century

The garden staff in 1999.
Back row (left to right):
Tony Bird, Heather Baker, Chris Hubbuck, Ian Fisher, Jim Link, Stefan Homerski, Tim Walton, Ian Webster, Glenn Facer, Peter Nowell, Richard Corcoran, Glenn Ashton, Rob Dowding, Jeff Madin.
Front row: Barrie Bateman, Barbara Burchby, Michael Shewen, Catriona Spillane, Ian Webster junior, Andrew Law, Colin Bright. (Matthew Bullen and Peter Blackwell were on holiday when the photograph was taken.)

records can never be repeated since the school-leaving age has been raised to sixteen. Now we look forward to Ian Webster's tenure of the garden he knows so well.

Andrew has nearly reached his own fifty years of responsibility for Chatsworth and so we have been here long enough to have seen some of our schemes come to fruition. But Miss Jekyll could have been describing Chatsworth in the second half of the twentieth century when she wrote 'there was no definite plan at the beginning. Various parts were taken in hand at different times and the whole afterwards reconciled as might be most suitably contrived'. From the roof you can see how the separate parts roughly thrown together have been reconciled in a comfortingly English muddle: the Elizabethan Hunting Tower on the hill, the 1st Duke's Greenhouse, Cascade and Canal of the 1690s, Paine's wondrous Stables of the 1760s and the Salisbury Lawns of the same time, Paxton's Conservative Wall of 1848, my mother-in-law's 1939 Rose Garden, the pleached limes, our Serpentine Hedge and Chiswick House pattern in the West Garden of the 1950s, the Display Greenhouse and my retina irritant of the 1970s, and the *War Horse, 1991* – four hundred years at a glance.

Future generations will no doubt change much of it, but that would not be unusual. Inhabited by its own family who have ensured that it is unfrozen and malleable is the reason this house and garden have stayed alive over the centuries.

People seem to like coming to a place which is lived in. They ask gardeners, wardens and the shop ladies about the incumbents and many find it hard to believe that anyone could be dotty enough to live in such a vast house. Last summer a keen questioner of the girl in the Information Room returned after a while to tell her 'I saw the Duchess in the garden' and added with some surprise, 'She looked quite normal ... really'.

One of the pleasures of living here is that people seem to become as attached to the place as we are, including those who like walking in the park and in the woods. Some come to the garden every week to enjoy the changing seasons. As well as enjoying the beauty of the landscape people tell us it is the freedom which appeals. All are welcome to bring their children and dogs into the park and garden to picnic where they like, play games, walk and run on the grass, make a noise and paddle in the Cascade if they wish. The result is a sort of loyalty to the place which makes our regular visitors treat it as their own. Often the relations of someone who has died ask Andrew if they can plant a tree in the park in their memory, or provide a seat for some favourite place. Thus the ties with our neighbours are strengthened. When asked if we mind the summer crowds the answer is definitely no. The house and garden are meant to be seen and enjoyed. Without people the place would be melancholy, bereft of what it was all made for. It is the visitors who make the cheerful atmosphere.

The Bachelor Duke must have the last word. His hospitable spirit is everywhere, indoors and out. Perhaps one day I will meet him on my endless walks along the two miles of Green Drive he made round his garden.

'I shall not undertake to lead you through the kitchen garden: the botanical treasures there require a more able and technical description than I can give, and the fruit-trees and vegetables, that rival them in perfection, would increase the difficulty of the task; but when you have been there, when you have visited the Stand and the new fountain-reservoir, when you have been round the four mile walk, and have examined the villages of Calton Lees and Edensor, paying great attention to the farm, you will have revived the most thorough acquaintance with Chatsworth and what surrounds it; and you will make allowances for the excess of pride, vanity, egotism — call it what you please — that have made me dwell upon such minute particulars in complying with your request. To enjoy such sources of happiness, and to see the pleasure they cause to others, would make it as impossible to treat them with indifference, as it is to deserve the possession of them.'

Andrew and myself by the stone seat on the West Drive in March 1999.

AUTHOR'S NOTE

In 1980, at the request of Andrew and our son, Peregrine (Stoker) Hartington, the Trustees of the Chatsworth Settlement granted a 99-year lease at a rent of £1 per annum of Chatsworth House, its essential contents, garden, park and some woods, a total of 1,569 acres, to a charitable foundation called Chatsworth House Trust, the object being the 'long-term preservation of Chatsworth for the benefit of the public'. An endowment fund was created from the sale of works of art from the private side of the house and from other family resources. The income from this trust fund goes towards the upkeep of the house, garden and park, which are now the responsibility of the Council of Management of Chatsworth House Trust. In 1994 an additional 253 acres were added to the lease.

The family is represented on the Council, but there is a majority of independent members. Andrew and his Trustees have never applied for a grant for restoration of the Grade 1 listed buildings leased to the House Trust, these buildings being maintained exclusively from the resources of the House Trust and the income from visitors.

Notes

Unless credited below, all the quotations in the text come from private archive material held at Chatsworth, including Chatsworth account books, correspondence and diaries of various Dukes of Devonshire, correspondence of Paxton, the *Handbook of Chatsworth and Hardwick* by the 6th Duke (privately printed in 1844), and the 6th Duke's scrapbook of the royal visit.

1 John Walker, August 1677, diarist (private collection unpublished)

2 Charles Cotton, *Wonders of the Peak*, 3rd edition 1715 (first published 1681 but probably written earlier)

3 White Kennet, sermon at 1st Duke's funeral, 1708

4 Stephen Switzer *The Nobleman, Gentleman and Gardener's Recreation*, 1715. Switzer was an English garden designer and writer.

5 W Carew Hazlitt *Gleanings in Old Garden Literature*, 1887

6 The garden at Melbourne Hall was planned by London and Wise for Thomas Coke about the same time, but the plans were not executed till some years later.

7 *The Illustrated Journeys of Celia Fiennes c.1682–c1712*, edited by Christopher Morris, 1982

8 Londesborough, in the East Riding of Yorkshire, was a property of the 3rd Earl of Burlington and was refurbished by him in the 1730s. It descended to the 6th Duke of Devonshire who, alas, pulled down the house in 1819 and sold the estate to George Hudson 'the railway king' in the 1840s.

9 Sir Godfrey Copley, in Dev Mss 1st Series 70.19

10 Daniel Defoe *A Tour through England & Wales —divided into Circuits or Journies*, Vol 2, 1927

11 Joseph Taylor (Late of the Inner Temple, Esq) *A Journey to Edenborough in Scotland*, 1903 edition

12 Defoe *op.cit.*

13 Francis Bickley *The Cavendish Family*, 1911, citing 'Memoirs of James, Earl Waldegrave'

14 Horace Walpole *The History of the Modern Taste in Gardening*, 1771–80

15 Alexander Pope *An Epistle to the Rt Hon Richard, Earl of Burlington, by Mr Pope*, 1731

16 The 4th Duke was MP 1741–51, called to the House of Lords as Baron Cavendish in 1751, succeeded as Duke in 1755, and was Prime Minister 1756–57.

17 Peter Cunningham *Letters of Horace Walpole*, Vol III, 1891

18 Francis Thompson 'A History of Chatsworth', *Country Life*, 1949 citing 'Walpole's Journal 1768' (Walpole Society XVI p65). Francis Thompson, 1886–1964, was librarian at Chatsworth for many years.

19 Defoe *op.cit.*

20 Thompson *op.cit.*

21 Dr O. L. Gilbert 'The ancient lawns at Chatsworth', *Journal of the Royal Horticultural Society*, December 1983

22 Thompson *op.cit.*

23 Lady Elizabeth Foster, 1759–1824, daughter of 4th Earl of Bristol, married John Foster in 1776, and was the bosom friend of Georgiana, Duchess of Devonshire. She was mistress of Georgiana's husband, the 5th Duke, by whom she had two children. This *ménage à trois* surprised even their contemporaries. After Georgiana's death Lady Elizabeth married the Duke.

24 Dev Mss 1st Series 675.330A

25 'To our son and brother Jean-Pierre. Much loved. 10 August 1956–13 October 1996'

26 Lady Blanche Howard, 1812–40, daughter of the 6th Earl of Carlisle and grand-daughter of Georgiana, and neice of the Bachelor Duke. In 1829 she married the 2nd Earl of Burlington (second creation), 1808-91, who became 7th Duke of Devonshire in 1858.

27 Princess Victoria's Journal Oct 20 1832, from The Royal Archives

28 Princess Victoria's Journal Oct 24 1832, from The Royal Archives

29 Basil & Jessie Harley *A Gardener at Chatsworth: three years in the life of Robert Aughtie 1848-1850*, 1992

30 The technical details are set out in *Magazine of Botany*, Vol 2, 1835, and Transactions of the Society of Arts, 57, 1850–51.

31 Miss Emily Eden was author of *Up the Country* and *Princes and People of India* etc.

33 Violet Markham, *Paxton and The Bachelor Duke*, 1935

34 W Adam *The Gem of the Peak*, 1851

35 W Adam *ibid.*

36 Frederick Burkhardt and Sydney Smith *The Correspondence of Charles Darwin, Vol 3, 1844–1846*, (date unknown) citing Mss 405A Smithsonian Institution Libraries, Washington DC 20560-0630

37 Queen Victoria's Journal 1 Dec 1843, from The Royal Archives

38 Queen Victoria's letter to King of the Belgians 4 Dec 1843, from The Royal Archives. Quoted in *The Letters of Queen Victoria. A selection from Her Majesty's correspondence between the years 1837 and 1861, Vol 1, 1837-1843*, edited by Arthur Christopher Benson and Viscount Esher, 1907

39 George Anson, Private Secretary to Prince Albert, memorandum 4 Dec 1843, from The Royal Archives

40 Dantan jeune (1800–69) was a French sculptor who visited London between 1833 and 1841 and caricatured a number of English subjects.

41 Basil & Jessie Harley *op.cit.*

42 *Magazine of Botany*, Vol V

43 *Magazine of Botany*, Vol XI

44 *The Gardener's Magazine*, 1831

45   *Derbyshire Courier, Chesterfield Gazette and General County Advertiser*, 30 June 1849

46   Basil & Jessie Harley *op.cit.*

47   *Gardeners' Chronicle*, 5 Sept 1874

48   Lady Frederick Cavendish, 1841-1925, daughter of 4th Baron Lyttleton, married Lord Frederick Cavendish in 1864. He was murdered in Phoenix Park, Dublin in 1882. Her diary entry 17 December 1842.

49   Patrick Jackson *The Last of the Whigs: A Political Biography of Lord Hartington, later 8th Duke of Devonshire (1833–1908)*, 1994.

50   Lady Maud Baillie 1896-1975, daughter of 9th Duke of Devonshire, author of *Early Memories*, privately printed in 1989.

51   Lady Maud Baillie *ibid.*

52   Kenneth Lemmon *The Covered Garden*, 1962

53   P. F. S. Poulson 'Spring in Spain, Summer in England', 1950. An account of his visit was sent privately to Chatsworth.

54   Francis Kingdon-Ward, 1885–1958, plant collector, botanist, explorer and author.

55   *The Handbook of British Flora* by George Bentham & revised by Sir J. Hooker, illustrations of the British Flora drawn by W. H. Fitch, 1930.

56   Clarence Elliott, 1881–1969, plant collector and writer.

57   Robert John Thornton *The Temple of Flora or Garden of Nature*, 1799–1807

58   Arthur Ronald Lambert Field Tree, 1897–1976, Master of Pytchley Hounds 1927–33, MP for Harborough, Leicestershire 1933–45, married Nancy Field (née Perkins, later Lancaster). Father of Michael Tree who married Lady Anne Cavendish.

59   Algernon Bertram Freeman-Mitford, 1st Baron Redesdale (2nd creation 1902), 1837–1916, diplomat, writer and gardener.

60   Alan Mitchell, 1922–95, dendrologist, author of *A Field Guide to the Trees of Britain and Northern Europe*, 1974.

61   Vicki Hallett, later Schilling, dendrologist, worked with Alan Mitchell and was driving force behind the formation of TROBI.

62   Dr Johnson 'Life of Pope'in *Lives of the most eminent English Poets*, Vol IV, a new edition corrected 1783

63   Note that there is no access to Stand Wood from the garden. The entrance is on the road to the Farmyard.

64   Henry Luttrell, 1765?–1851, wit and poet, and friend of Georgiana, Duchess of Devonshire.

Index

Page numbers in *italics* refer to the captions to illustrations

Acknowledgements

I would like to thank Her Majesty the Queen for her gracious permission to quote from the Journals of Queen Victoria and Sheila de Bellaigue for her kindness in finding the relevant passages in the Royal Archives.

I would also like to thank all who have so kindly given me permission to quote from the sources listed in the notes.

I would like to thank Frances Lincoln for suggesting the book and Tristram Holland, my editor, for her endless good advice (and for many hours spent in the train to and from Chesterfield). She put disorder into order in the kindest possible way. Prue Bucknall, Caroline Hillier and Tristram solved the jigsaw puzzle of text and pictures. I thank Gary Rogers for his incomparable photographs. He has brought a new eye to a much photographed place and we are all grateful for this.

Jim Link has followed in his father's footsteps, loved and respected by all. He always says yes to impossible requests. Ian Webster knows everything about his greenhouse plants and has answered many questions. Barbara Burchby gave quick answers to more questions from her potting shed office.

Peter Day, Charles Noble and Tom Askey found all kinds of essential stuff in the bowels of the Chatsworth muniment room and elsewhere in the house.

Ian Else and James Trevethick gave me accurate measurements of boundaries, paths, hedges, lakes, ponds and lawns.

Diane Naylor found and checked the weather books. Sue Band has carried heavy books along passages unknown to man.

Anita Page and Trudy Roe explained the mysteries of the nomenclature of plants. Anne Coates spotted relevant entries in the diaries of the 6th and 7th Dukes of Devonshire. Louise Ingham battled with the 6th Duke's handwriting to find references to plants and the garden.

Ian Fraser-Martin took photographs to add to our vast store based on Chatsworth house, garden and collection.

Simon Seligman is a very present help in time of trouble.

Alan Bell of The London Library immediately found a badly needed book so dim it hardly exists.

Laurence Knighton, Mayor of Bakewell, knows everything about railways and their history and told me what I wanted to know.

Ralph Kerr explained what London and Wise did for the garden at Melbourne Hall.

David Cook, Keeper of the Palm House at Kew, showed me the Amherstia nobilis.

Colin Morgan, curator of Bedgebury National Pinetum, spent two cold days in December identifying trees in the Pinetum.

Nicholas Smith of Currey & Co, solicitors, did not complain when parcels of pine needles and cones arrived at his office for further identification.

Pamela Stevenson, secretary of The Tree Register of the British Isles, asked David Alderman, Trustee of TROBI, for help on this vexed subject, which was willingly given.

Michael and Anne Tree reminded me of the iron four poster bed covered in a vine and the chair covered in a rambling rose, ideas invented by them which prompted me to embellish the Cottage Garden.

Hal Bagot of beautiful Levens Hall allowed me to quote the long service records of the head gardeners there.

My daughter Emma painted the camellia illustrated below.

Nearer home there is Helen Marchant. Without her there would be no book. Her patience and constant good humour and the speed and accuracy of her work combined to encourage me on. My gratitude to her is unbounded.

D.D.

PUBLISHER'S ACKNOWLEDGEMENTS

All photographs by Gary Rogers except those on the following pages:
Bill Burlington 78 (below), Country Life Picture Library 66, Ian Fraser-Martin 94 (above and below), Jerry Harpur 159 (above), Andrew Lawson 42 and 109 (centre and right below), Christopher Simon Sykes 39 (right). All historic material by courtesy of the Trustees of the Chatsworth Settlement.
Map illustration on the endpapers by Joanna Logan.
The publishers thank Derbyshire Countryside for the family tree, Tony Lord for his help with plant names, and Stephen Hayward for the index.

Art Editor Prue Bucknall
Production Hazel Kirkman
Picture Editor Anne Fraser
Art Director Caroline Hillier
Editorial Director Kathryn Cave

Emma Tennant '99

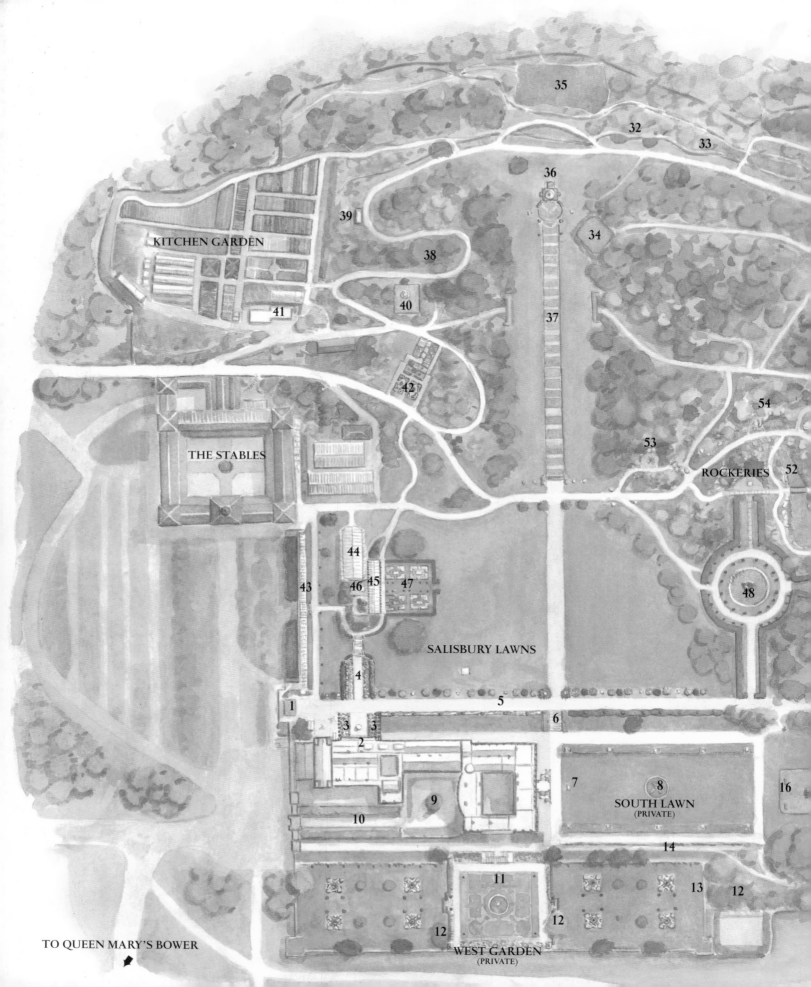

35

32

33

36

39

KITCHEN GARDEN

38

34

41

40

37

54

42

53

THE STABLES

ROCKERIES

52

44

45

46

43

47

48

SALISBURY LAWNS

4

1

5

6

3   3

2

7   8

16

9

SOUTH LAWN
(PRIVATE)

10

14

11

13   12

12

TO QUEEN MARY'S BOWER

12

WEST GARDEN
(PRIVATE)